¡HOLA TEQUILA!

For Shannon . . . thank you.

Published by Sellers Publishing, Inc.

Sellers Publishing, Inc.
161 John Roberts Road, South Portland, Maine 04106
Visit our Web site: www.sellerspublishing.com
E-mail: rsp@rsvp.com

ISBN 13: 978-1-4162-0691-0
e-ISBN: 978-1-4162-0731-3
Library of Congress Control Number: 2011935642

¡HOLA TEQUILA!

Ninety creative cocktails and inspired shooters

BY COLLEEN GRAHAM

Photography by
Shannon Graham

SELLERS
PUBLISHING

Contents

introduction

Tequila. It is one of the six "base" distilled spirits essential to the modern bar; it has a notorious reputation; it has been around for centuries; it was the first liquor produced in North America; it has been considered both a Gift from the Gods and the Devil's Elixir; it makes a margarita a margarita. It is, simply, tequila. There is no other beverage that can contend with it in notoriety — simultaneously shady and respectable — or taste, and it cannot be mistaken. This is the beauty and the enigma of tequila.

For years, tequila has been put on the back burner of the bar. Over its integration with the Mexican culture, there were many periods when it was the "poor man's drink," not sophisticated enough for the aristocracy spoiled by European imports. In the U.S. it has a notorious reputation as the "partier's" drink, reserved for frat parties and occasions when everyone just wants to get "wasted." How often have you been visiting a friend's home, and they walk to the bar mid-conversation while asking, "Can I get you a glass of tequila?" as if it were some prized bourbon they received for their birthday? Unless your friend is a tequila aficionado, the chances of this happening are unlikely. Furthermore, many people throughout the world had not heard of — much less tasted — tequila until a rather recent increase in international exports.

Many of us have a love-hate relationship with tequila. The "hate" aspect can frequently be attributed to a single experience from college days or the like, involving one too many. I cannot begin to count the number of people who have told me, "I just can't do tequila anymore." When I probe into their reasoning — typically while a whiskey and Coke, a martini, or other strong drink sits before them — they recount one of "those" nights and have sworn off tequila ever since. Well, the tequila many of these people encountered does not reflect the state of tequila in today's market, even if it was just a decade ago. After a bit of cajoling, I can often reintroduce the infamous liquor to them, and they don't look back on that night.

On the other hand, there is a growing number of tequila enthusiasts throughout the world. These imbibers have found a love for the Mexican liquor that rivals many a Scotch connoisseur. Their taste for tequila is a passion, and they'll go to any lengths to find something new and different, obscure and unknown. Some could tell you in a blind tasting if the tequila came from the area around the town of Tequila, the highlands of Jalisco, or one of the other five Mexican states legally permitted to produce tequila.

Times have changed for tequila. It has evolved in so many ways over the last few decades that it is now a product associated with civility, a refined liquor for the enlightened. Tequila has grown up to meet the demands of the consumer. It has been reborn, has found a ritzier side, and its image has been polished up just like any old ragamuffin brought in from the streets and given a bath, a new set of clothes, and some lessons in good taste. Tequila is no longer a dirty word, nor is it taboo.

Tequila has also evolved inside the mixed drink. It was not until the middle of the 20th century that it found a place in bars outside of Mexico. Prior to that, it would frequently be hidden under layers of fruit juices or heavy liqueurs, or relegated to lie in wait for the next round of celebratory shots or the next, oft poorly made, margarita. Today we're infusing tequilas; we use it with herbs and fresh, exotic fruits and high-end liqueurs, and whatever else imaginative mixologists can concoct. We are no longer disguising our tequila's unique piquancy; we are celebrating it, finding brand-new complements, and proudly displaying our favorite bottles alongside that coveted, though less often used, XO brandy.

If you have the opportunity and want to enhance your tequila experiences, I suggest going straight to the source. My trips to the Mexican distilleries and agave fields strengthened my appreciation for the spirit tenfold, and I was able to return home with fascinating stories of the people behind the scenes and the methods they use, which are often steeped in centuries of tradition. The tequila country within Jalisco alone is diverse. Simply flying into Guadalajara, you can see acres of blue dotting the landscape below; when you hit the town of Tequila, you will find roadside vendors lining the streets and distilleries rich with history, complete with century-old haciendas and a drier style of tequila. Traveling up to Los Altos around the town of Arandas, you will find richer tequilas, and many times get a sense of modernism in the distilleries there. Each tequila distillery and region has a life of its own that is a unique character as diverse as their tequilas.

On your journey, which many tour and travel agencies can help arrange, you cannot pass up the opportunity to walk through an agave field. It is one of the most serene places you will find on Earth — wide open, neatly planted rows of giant blue succulents for as far as the eye can see. If you're lucky, the *jimadores* will be harvesting that day, and you can witness a giant *piña* emerge from the ground, and maybe even try your hand at shearing its leaves using a traditional coa (a tool used for harvesting). Tequila is one of the most labor-intensive distilled spirits in the world, and it begins in the fields on a scale that you cannot imagine until you experience it for yourself.

And so, I invite you to journey with me through a visit to the world of tequila. We will get to know her better, admire her progress, and learn how to use her to her fullest potential. Tequila is one of the most fascinating, diverse, and culturally enhanced beverages available, and along with all the people who have crafted her over the years, is deserving of our respect and appreciation.

comencemos, salud

Equivalents

½ fl. oz. = 15 ml (1 tbsp.)

1 fl. oz. = 30 ml (2 tbsp.)

2 fl. oz. = 60 ml (4 tbsp. or ¼ cup)

Note: These conversions have been slightly rounded for measuring convenience.

1 dash = 6 drops

standard shot glass = 1.5 fl. oz.

short "pony" shot glass = 1 fl. oz.

acknowledgments

The first person I must thank is my talented husband and business partner, Shannon. He has been my rock and support through our many adventures over the years and, as my primary taste tester, has endured many cocktail experiments with a smile and an honest opinion. He has also supplied the beautiful photography in this book, and for that I am truly grateful.

My family and friends are due a big thank-you and a round of hugs for their support and advice, which have become an invaluable part of who I am today.

A hearty "Cheers!" must go out to all of my colleagues at About.com and in the cocktail community. I am continually learning from all of you and greatly appreciate and value every one of our friendships. When it comes to tequila specifically, I must thank the people at the Tequila Regulatory Council and Distilled Spirits Council of the United States, the hospitable distillers in Mexico, and my contacts throughout the tequila industry for the fantastic experiences and knowledge from which I have created much of this material, in hopes of passing along a love of tequila. As a whole, I believe we can continue to encourage the newfound respect for both tequila and cocktails, so everyone can enjoy a better drink.

Furthermore, I would like to thank Robin Haywood and Sellers Publishing for pursuing this book and for all of their support. The wonderful people at Montage in Cedar Falls, Iowa, deserve kudos for allowing us to photograph in their stunning restaurant.

Lastly, I feel the need to thank every single one of my readers who have faithfully taken in my articles, blogs, and recipes over the years, shared their experiences, asked questions, and given me useful feedback. Without all of you, I would not be writing this today, and for those who encouraged me to pursue a book, well, here you go.

salud

*Mariachi dancers performing at San Nicholas,
home of Tequila Corazon distillery*

CHAPTER 1:

Types of Tequila

███ █ ██ ██ ████ █ ██ █

oday's tequila is defined and protected by its Appellation of Origin in the same way as some brandies (e.g., Cognac) and wines (e.g., Burgundy or Champagne). Regulations have been developed and enforced by the Consejo Regular del Tequila (CRT, or Tequila Regulatory Council). They go like this:

The categories of tequila — *Tequila 100% de Agave* and *Tequila* — are based on the species of agave used to produce the liquor. *Tequila 100% de Agave* must be produced entirely of Weber blue agave (*Agave tequilana*) and be bottled at the source. Within this category are the highest-quality tequilas, which will be clearly indicated on the bottle. *Tequila* (or mixto), on the other hand, needs only 51% Weber blue agave, with other species of agave making up the remainder. The other option within this category is that it can or cannot be bottled in Mexico, a useful clause for producers with bottling facilities in other countries. Some good tequilas can be found in this category as well and, up until a few years ago, this category led in exports and production.

Once the category has been determined, tequila can be further classified into one of five classes (or *tipos*). These are found in both categories and are essentially a designation of age and the presence or absence of additives.

TYPE 1 *Blanco*

Blanco (also called Silver, Plata, or White) tequila is the purest of tequilas. This is where you will get a taste of unadulterated, additive-free agave. These tequilas are not aged, spending, at most, 60 days in stainless-steel tanks for storage. As the name implies, these are clear-colored tequilas and are the foundation for the other classes. One may find *blanco suave* on tequila labels; this is used by some brands to distinguish their blanco as smoother (*muy suave*) than a typical blanco. Many blancos are smooth (especially *100% de*

Agave) and are ideal for straight tequila shots and any mixed drink you would like to throw them in.

TYPE 2 *Joven*

This type of tequila is referred to as joven ("young" in Spanish) or *oro* ("gold") tequila. It is a silver tequila that has been colored or flavored with at least one of the following (more often the first, but a combination can be used): caramel color, oak natural extracts, glycerin, or sugar syrup. Gold tequilas fit into the "its taste is softened without aging" clause of that official tequila definition. These are also the tequilas that were, more often than not, responsible for bad tequila experiences among individual drinkers, as they were the most widely distributed in the United States until recent times, and are known to have a distinct bite, particularly a "burn" in the finish. Think of jovens as having the look of age without the years — a teenager trying to pass as an adult.

A section of a large mural located at Mundo Cuervo, Jalisco, Mexico, the maker of José Cuervo tequila. The mural honors the history of the tequila from harvesting the agave to distillation.

Appellation of Origin

Appellation of Origin is the definition of standards set for a particular product. In 1978, the tequila industry first registered the official standards with the World Industrial Property Organization (WIPO). From that time, to be labeled as "tequila" the liquor must meet the Official Standard for Tequila, known as NOM-006-SCFI-2005 (the updated declaration as of 2011). Part of the regulation states that tequila may be produced only in certain municipalities in the following Mexican states: 124 municipalities of Jalisco, 8 municipalities of Nayarit, 7 municipalities of Guanajuato, 30 municipalities of Michoacán, and 11 municipalities of Tamaulipas.

TYPE 3 *Reposado*

Back to the "additive-free" tequilas: reposados are "rested" tequilas. These popular tequilas take a siesta of sorts for at least two months in oak barrels before bottling, with some of the higher-end reposados receiving three to nine months. This is where we begin to taste the mellowing effects of aging via wood. These tend to have a subtle oaky undertone that softens the raw agave flavor while maintaining a robust, earthy flavor. As the "middle ground" of tequila types, reposados can be used in most mixed drinks, are best in cocktails with light flavors, and are enjoyable to sip straight.

TYPE 4 *Añejo*

Añejo tequilas are like a well-aged whiskey. This "aged" class must be barreled in wood for at least one year, though many go longer, with some of the best spending four years in oak and jumping up to the next class. A sip of a fine añejo can redefine almost anyone's perception of tequila. It is often a perfect marriage of earthy agave and wood, packaged into an ultra-smooth liquor in which you can find butterscotch and caramel notes. Añejos are best served chilled or on the rocks and can be used in delicate cocktails for a sophisticated complement.

TYPE 5 *Extra-Añejo*

These tequilas are a sort of subclass of añejos and encompass those tequilas aged for three or more years. In extra-añejos — or *muy* añejos — you will find tequilas that can rival 30-year-old whiskies and come with a price tag that reflects this fact. Save the extra-añejos for special occasions, and enjoy them slowly in a well-chilled brandy snifter that allows you to fully appreciate their seniority.

Reserva de Casa
This special class of tequilas is often an extra-añejo that is very limited in production. They can be considered the ultra-refined version of tequilas. Reserva de casa can also be referred to as *gran reposado* or *reserva de la familia*, depending on the brand.

Flavored Tequilas
In recent years quite a few tequila producers have released flavored tequilas. These are infused tequilas, often blancos, with flavors that range from exotic fruits to hot peppers. Though commercially made flavored tequilas are not as popular as vodkas, they are beginning to catch on, and many consumers are experimenting with creating their own unique infusions. See page 31 for more on homemade tequila infusions.

Other Agave Products

It is important to briefly mention agave-based products that are similar to tequila, but which are not technically tequila, as you may run across them in your adventures. Very few of these are available commercially outside of their home regions, but this may be useful information as you travel Mexico.

The Cost of Tequila
In general, tequila is not what many would consider inexpensive liquor. Can you find a $10 bottle of tequila? Maybe, but I would seriously question its quality. Tequila production is one of the most labor-intensive of all spirits, with much of it done by "hand," and the end cost often reflects that. While you can find tequilas at most price points, it is typical that gold tequilas are the least expensive, followed by blanco, then the aged spirits. The longer tequila stays in the barrel, the more you are going to pay. In this very broad market you can expect to pay $20–$50 for 750ml of premium tequila, though specialty bottlings can run up to a few hundred U.S. dollars.

Reading the Label

Much can be learned about a certain tequila by reading its label. First, it must have the word *Tequila,* the class (blanco, reposado, etc.), and the liquor's designation as either *Tequila* or *Tequila 100% de Agave.* To designate the producer, the initials *NOM (Norma Oficial Mexicana* or Official Mexican Standard) and a four-digit number unique to each distillery are required, often alongside the initials *CRT.* The address of either the producer or bottler, the lot number of the tequila, and two statements — one that it is a "Product of Mexico," and the other a warning about the potential harms of drinking — along with alcohol by volume and net contents in liters must also appear on the label. If any of those elements is missing, or if there is no label whatsoever, it is not recommended to buy that tequila as it's likely counterfeit.

Pulque

The main difference between pulque, tequila, and mezcal is that the agave sap is not cooked prior to fermentation when making pulque, whereas in tequila and mezcal the sap, or juice, is derived from baked agave. Pulque has been used as a nutritional supplement recently, because it contains proteins, vitamins, and carbohydrates, and some claim that it is one of the most nutritionally beneficial alcoholic drinks. However, nutrients are not all of the extras one could find in pulque over the years. In the past, some pulque producers added intoxicating herbs or employed a trick or two to speed fermentation. The most daring of these was dunking a *muñeca* (rag doll) filled with human feces into the brew. While the practice is long gone, the story remains and continues to tarnish pulque's reputation.

Pulque was very common in Mexico until recently, though it can still be found as a home brew in some rural and tourist areas. Occasionally, one can find it commercially in a six-pack of cans, but it does not store well. If you get the opportunity, pulque is worth trying, not so much for the taste (which many have described as having a gasoline quality), as for the historical experience.

Jimador harvests agave piña at San Nicolas distillery near Arandas, Mexico

Tequila Is a Mezcal, Mezcal Is Not a Tequila

"Mezcal" is commonly used to define any agave-based distilled spirit, with the exception of liqueurs, which have sugar additives, among other things. With this definition, tequila, sotol, and bacanora are all mezcals. However, mezcal is *not* tequila, because it is not made exclusively (or at least 51%) of Weber blue agave and does not have to be produced in the designated states and municipalities required of tequila and protected in the Appellation of Origin. This is similar to the fact that all Cognac is brandy, but all brandy is not Cognac. Tequila and Cognac are merely regionally distinct subclasses of mezcal and brandy, respectively.

Mezcal

Mezcal is not a common name outside of Mexico, but one aspect of it is very familiar — the worm, or *gusano*. To get one thing straight immediately, good mezcal does not include a worm or any other creepy crawly creature. It is also a common misconception that tequilas include this novelty, when all along it has been mezcal. The worm is said to be proof of the alcohol's strength, because it can preserve the undamaged larva of one of two moths that live on agave plants.

Another distinguishing fact about the name mezcal is that it is often used to describe all agave-based distilled spirits. Similar to the brandy-Cognac relationship, all tequila is mezcal, but all mezcal is not tequila by law. Tequila is particularly defined by its Appellation of Origin (as Cognac is), and that is the basic distinction.

Mezcal by definition is a liquor distilled from any of 28 varieties of agave, 90% of which is *Agave angustifolia*. In 1994, regulations similar to those imposed on tequila were established, and regions were designated for its production. The majority today comes from the state of Oaxaca. Mezcal is often made in small batches from one of approximately 500 mostly rural distilleries; three of those operate on a large commercial scale.

Mezcal production continues to employ traditional methods. One is the practice of roasting the piñas in rock-lined pits. This gives the liquor its characteristic flavor, which is smoky and can be off-putting to some people. If you enjoy a smoky Scotch, give mezcal a try. I have had some excellent mezcals and have tasted a fair share of harshly horrible ones as well. It is definitely a spirit that is either a winner or a loser, and it may take time to develop a palate for it. Sadly, it can be difficult to find those great premium mezcals, though they are becoming more readily available. Some of this is due to tequila aficionados, with a disdain for tequila's newfound commercialism, switching over to seek out a more authentic Mexican spirit.

A classic Oaxacan drink is Donají, a mix of mezcal and orange juice on ice with grenadine floating on top. It is served in a glass rimmed with chili powder and salt and garnished with an orange.

Sotol

A regional mezcal from Chihuahua, sotol is made from a non-agave succulent called dasylirion and is often aged for six months. Sotol is usually not available outside of the region.

A section of a large mural located at Mundo Cuervo, Jalisco, Mexico, the maker of José Cuervo tequila. The mural honors the history of the tequila from harvesting the agave to distillation.

LA PUERTA VERDE
MEXICO

Raicilla

Raicilla (pronounced "rye-see-yah," and often called Mexican moonshine) has origins in Jalisco and is now concentrated around Puerta Vallarta, making it a local treat for tourists. It is made from *Agave inaequidens* (commonly known as *lechuguilla*) and until recently was an outlaw alcohol, bootlegged to avoid restrictions and taxes. Raicilla is not widely available commercially and remains more of a home-brew, small-batch spirit.

It is popular to drink raicilla straight, on the rocks, or with grapefruit soda.

Bacanora

Bacanora is similar to raicilla, but is made in the state of Sonora and was illegal until 1992. It is produced from the *Agave pacifica* (or *Agave yaquiana*), which is roasted in underground, lava rock–lined pits. Bacanora is typically available only in the northern Mexican region.

More Agave Spirits

There are more agave-based alcoholic beverages produced throughout the world, including the U.S. and South Africa. These are called "agave spirits," as they cannot technically take the name tequila or mezcal because of the Appellation of Origin declarations. Despite the legal distinctions of all of the agave-based spirits, you will find them grouped with tequila at the liquor store and particularly when shopping online.

Tequila continues to see a growth in use in liqueurs. Its unique flavor characteristics lend very well as a base for a variety of flavors. Any tequila-based liqueurs will be clearly identified as such on the label.

One other use of the name tequila should also be noted here, and that is "tequila-flavored" beverages. Beer and tequila are a common example, though there are other products that add the word *tequila* (or some derivation thereof) to their label in hopes of boosting their marketability. More often than not, this "tequila flavoring" is simply agave nectar (see page 30), but "agave flavor" just wouldn't have the name recognition that "tequila flavor" has. However, if you do enjoy the taste of agave, an agave beer every now and then is not a bad idea. On very rare occasions, these products may include actual tequila.

Tasting Tequila

Armed with the knowledge of tequila categories and classes, one can begin exploring the varieties of flavor possible from a single product. Though there are similarities in tequilas, the generalities of flavor are just that, general. Each brand will be unique, sometimes in subtle and often in forthright ways, from others. Countless factors play into a finished tequila — from the region where the agave are grown and the amount of sun or the soil content there, to the ovens, waters, yeasts, and woods used in its production — so much so that no two tequilas are identical.

Of the more than 1,300 brands of tequila produced (as of June 2011), many will create a range that includes a blanco, a reposado, and an añejo. This offers us, the consumers, a splendid opportunity to explore tequilas of various ages side by side. It is likely, though not guaranteed, that this trifecta from a single brand is distilled from the same plants or in the same region and, aside from aging, using the same production techniques.

For comparisons sake, grab a bottle of each type from one brand and smell and taste them individually, beginning with the blanco and working through to the añejo. Notice the raw, sweet agave of the blanco, the appearance of oak in the reposado, and the smooth, mellow saccharine of the añejo. What similarities do you notice that may be indicative of the brand, region, or distillery? Do this with some friends and see what they think. Throw in another brand or two to find characteristics that are different or similar. I've always found tequila to be perfect for this intriguing adventure in style, as each contains subtle nuances simultaneously characteristic of its brand and type.

Tequila flights are a common way to taste a variety of tequilas. These are often served in caballitos, or tall shot glasses, and displayed to the consumer in a row or on a tray.

When tasting tequila individually, a brandy snifter, old-fashioned glass, or wine glass is common. The key is to use a glass that is slightly tapered at the top, which allows the fragrance to become ensconced inside the glass. In 2002, the Reidel company designed a specific style of tequila-tasting glass made from the fine crystal that is their signature. This glass has become the standard for official tequila tasting.

Tequila tasting is similar to tasting other distilled spirits and wines. We examine the color and viscosity, take in the fragrance, and sip while noting the nuances of the entry, how it sits on the tongue, and the finish. After a few sips, we can begin to notice the subtleties found in tequila. You may recognize undertones of oak, butterscotch, or caramel in the aged tequilas, and a degree of raw agave and floral, herbal, and pepper tones in the younger tequilas.

The most poignant revelation many people find as they explore tequilas is that many lack a "bite." This is the burn found in many cheap liquors that takes you aback, causing a shudder throughout your body and leaving you feeling as if you could breathe fire unaided. In years past, this aspect of the finish of tequila deterred many from trying it again. Granted, there are many tequilas that will cause these reactions, but there are just as many with a surprisingly smooth finish preceded by a delicious taste. You should not have to recover from a sip of tequila; if you find that you do, it may be best to move on.

CHAPTER 2:

The Tequila Bar

Tequila is essential in any modern well-stocked bar. A bottle of blanco or gold, and more often a reposado, can be found alongside the whiskies, vodkas, gins, and rums in almost any commercial bar's liquor lineup. As tequila's popularity has grown, so have the tequila and mezcal bars that are opening up worldwide. In these establishments, tequila is at the forefront of the menu, and the tequila lover can have a field day.

When it comes to stocking your home bar, there isn't much difference between one that focuses on tequila and one with a standard stock. My recommendation for a well-rounded bar includes:

- **Whiskey:** bourbon, Canadian, rye, Scotch, and Irish
- **Vodka**
- **Gin**
- **Rum:** light and dark
- **Brandy**
- **Tequila:** blanco, reposado, and añejo
- **Liqueurs:** amaretto, coffee, chocolate, black raspberry, ginger, herb, orange, nut, vanilla (the flavors are generic; some of the most popular brands, such as Chambord, Navan, and Frangelico, would fall into these categories)
- **Sweet and dry vermouth**
- **Aromatic and orange bitters**
- **Sodas:** club soda (or seltzer, mineral water, or soda water), cola, ginger ale, tonic
- **Juices:** cranberry, grapefruit, lime, lemon, orange, pineapple, tomato
- **Other mixers:** grenadine, hot sauce, coffee, milk, simple syrup
- **Garnishes:** lemon, lime, cherry, olive, orange, pineapple, sugar, salt

A tequila-centered bar will include the standard juices, garnishes, liqueurs, and the base spirits noted above, just like any other bar. However, there are a few key ingredients that tequila cocktail devotees will want to consider stocking on a regular basis:

- Grapefruit juice and soda
- Orange liqueur (a variety)
- Fresh lemon, lime, orange, and grapefruit
- Bar salt for rimming
- Agave nectar
- Hot peppers and hot sauce
- Chocolate or grapefruit bitters

Those are just a few recommendations, because they either make a regular appearance in tequila cocktails or are natural complements to tequila. As you explore this spirit and develop your preferences, some may get knocked off your essential list, only to be replaced with other favorites.

I heartily recommend that every bar — tequila, commercial, or home — stock at least one each of a blanco, reposado, and añejo. The blanco will find the most use in cocktails; the reposado is ideal in light-flavored cocktails, shooters, and as a sipper; and the añejo will find a place in your heart as a nightcap, lazy afternoon sipper, or for use in select cocktails.

That said, I am not of the belief that añejos (or any well-aged liquor) should be designated solely for the purpose of the "sophisticated" neat sipping drink. Instead, I believe that if it is handled with care, there is nothing wrong with mixing añejo tequila in cocktails. Granted, I would not "waste" its smooth flavor in a blended margarita or other drinks with heavily flavored mixers, because the austerity

triple sec & other orange liqueurs

Orange liqueur should be simple, right? One would think so, but orange liqueur is deceptive, and an entire book could be dedicated to examining this subject. It is an important one, because these liqueurs are the most used fruit liqueurs in the bar. Basically, there are three styles, though they are often interchanged: triple sec, curaçao, and Cognac based. Triple sec is often clear and means *triple distilled* or *dry*. The very inexpensive, semi-generic bottles of triple sec are common to see, though some premium brands such as Cointreau and Combier are preferred. Curaçao is made from dried orange peels and originated on the small Caribbean island of the same name. It is a fun liqueur to play with, as it can be clear, orange, blue, and even green. Blue curaçao is a common way to make blue-colored drinks (see the blue margarita recipe variation on page 36). Then, there are the Cognac- or brandy-based orange liqueurs, the most popular of which is Grand Marnier. These will have a darker, richer flavor than other orange liqueurs. To add more confusion to the mix, some curaçaos have a brandy base.

Which liqueur should you use? Cocktail recipes typically include a suggestion; however, the choice is ultimately up to you. Some people love a margarita with triple sec, while others prefer the brandy version. For versatility's sake, I recommend stocking at least one light base and one brandy base in your bar.

of the añejo would be lost. On the other hand, a tequini made with añejo tequila, sweet vermouth, and grapefruit bitters, or an añejo paired with the simple freshness of fruits in the mode of the kiwi-strawberry rustico is perfectly acceptable, even preferred. Be picky about *how* aged spirits are used, not about a nonexistent rule that they should never touch a mixed drink. Tequila is far too much fun for such foolishness.

Bar Tools & Techniques

There are a few basic tools and techniques you will find useful when mixing cocktails. Some are necessary, and others are more of a luxury that can make your bartending experience easier.

Tools

Cocktail shaker: Two styles of cocktail shakers are available. One style, simply referred to as a "cocktail shaker," is the more common and easier to use, especially for beginners. It is a single, typically stainless-steel container, with a two-part lid comprised of a tight-fitting top with a built-in strainer and a small cap for covering the strainer while shaking.

The other style is called a Boston shaker and is often the choice of professional bartenders. These include a metal tin and a slightly smaller mixing glass which fits upside down inside the tin. When using a Boston shaker, it is best to pour the ingredients into the glass in order to see the proportions, fill the tin with ice, then pour the liquid from the glass over the ice before securing it in the tin to create a tight, leak-proof seal. When shaking, hold both vessels in case they come apart, and if they get stuck after shaking — which they often do because of the cold temperature — give the metal a firm tap against the counter edge to release the seal. Never hit the glass on the counter, as it can shatter. Shakers should be cleaned between drinks to prevent flavors from crossing into the next drink.

Hawthorne strainer: This strainer is required when using a Boston shaker, to prevent ice and any solid drink elements (i.e., fruit or herbs) from going into the finished drink. It is designed for one-handed straining, with a flat top, a coil of wire around the perimeter underneath, and a long handle. Place the coil inside the shaker's metal tin, grip the tin firmly and place your forefinger on top of the strainer, then tip the tin upside down over the glass until it is full.

Jigger: Jiggers are used to measure liquids, and until you are skilled with how much to pour for each ingredient, it is highly recommended that you use this handy device in order to create consistent cocktails. The jigger is made up of two cones on opposite ends; each has a different measurement that is usually inscribed in the metal or plastic. The standard jigger will measure 1 shot, or 1 ½ fluid ounces, on one end, and ½ shot, or ¾ fluid ounce on the other, though some jiggers use 2 and 1 fluid ounces, or 1 and ½ fluid ounces, for more precise measuring, and are great to have as well.

Bar spoon: The bar spoon is a long-handled stainless-steel spoon specifically designed for mixing drinks. The shaft is often twisted for easy stirring, and the spoon is narrow and often includes holes for pouring ingredients through. Its long shaft is designed to reach the depths of tall vessels often found in the bar, including shakers and garnish jars. A quality bar spoon will be your best friend in the bar.

Muddler: I love to muddle, which is apparent by the number of recipes included here that employ this simple tool, and I believe a good muddler is essential in the bar. Muddlers are like small batons, just long enough to reach the bottom of a standard cocktail shaker or a tall glass. Many are made of tapered wood, maxing out to around 1 ½ inches in diameter, and look like miniature baseball bats. Other muddlers are plastic, and some of these have teeth on the bottom that are ideal when mashing fruit. I choose to stock both, using the wood for most purposes, especially with herbs, and the plastic for fruits such as berries that stain the wood, or on cherries that have a tougher skin to puncture.

Speed pourer: A convenient replacement for the bottle's cap, it is used for frequently poured liquors. Some have an airtight seal and can be left in place, but with those that do not, it is important to replace the original cap when not using the liquor for significant periods of time. When you get good at using a speed pourer, you can use a 1-2-3 count to measure a full shot and avoid using a jigger. Some pourers are designed to automatically pour one measured shot on each tip of the bottle.

Ice tools: Ice is the most important ingredient in the bar and is used in almost every drink you will make. While not a requirement, tools for handling ice are nice to have around. This would include an ice bucket, scoop, and tongs. For crushing ice, a Lewis bag is handy (though a clean towel will do). Fill the bag with ice cubes, grab a muddler, and whack away until your ice is crushed to your liking.

Juicer: You will notice that I talk about fresh juice in many of the recipes, and this is because fresh ingredients make superior-tasting cocktails. You can take juicing to an extreme and buy an electric juicer to turn any fresh fruit into a liquid instantly. That is great and I do recommend it, but if it does not work within your budget or space limitations, the least you can do is get a handheld citrus juicer. These range in size, and I like the handled lever presses designed for lemons because they work for limes as well, and those two fruits are the most common to use in the small amounts these presses produce. Simply place a half of the fruit in the open cup, close it up, and press the handles together until you get the amount of juice desired.

Blender: Essential for frozen cocktails.

Soda siphon: An old-fashioned soda siphon is a luxury that replaces the need to stock bottles of club soda or mineral water. Fill the tank with distilled water, insert a CO_2 cartridge, and press the lever to release fresh soda into your drinks.

Knives and cutting board: In order to cut garnishes, you will need sharp paring knives and a cutting board. Keep these clean in between uses.

Grater or zester: These small tools do not take up much room and are great for adding lemon zest or grated chocolate, nutmeg, or cinnamon to the top of drinks.

Corkscrew and bottle opener: Few things are more frustrating than not being able to open a bottle because you do not have the proper tool. Consider both a corkscrew and a bottle opener essential in your bar.

Stir sticks, straws, napkins, and coasters: These items will make serving your drinks easier. Sticks and straws allow the drinker to stir their drinks, especially tall ones, as ingredients settle over time. Napkins and coasters placed under each glass keep your bar or table clean and save you time later.

Techniques

As you browse through the recipes in this book, you will find tips for these techniques that are specific to making that particular drink. Below is the general procedure for many of the common bartending techniques used.

Shaking: Many drinks are shaken, and it is very easy, though I see it done halfway far too often. When you shake a cocktail you want to fully integrate all of the ingredients, and this is done best by vigorously shaking the shaker up and down while holding both pieces of the shaker for security. Do this for about ten seconds, or until the metal of the shaker gets nice and frosty. Shake longer if using thick ingredients like milk or eggs, to ensure the proper mixing of ingredients. We typically hold the shaker over our shoulder (which one usually depends on if you are right or left handed), with the top facing backward just in case it spills, because it is better for a bartender to have a wet backside than for a customer or guest to be covered in liquor. If you shake a cocktail and it is to be served over ice, use fresh ice in the glass.

Stirring: Stirring is used most often for cocktails that are made up solely of alcohol and for tall drinks served over ice. The key to stirring drinks is to be gentle and to allow the ingredients to integrate slowly. Hold the spiral of the bar spoon between the thumb and forefinger, and twist it back and forth for about 30 seconds. As with shaking, in most cases you will strain over fresh ice in the serving glass.

Muddling: Muddling is used to combine ingredients, often solids such as herbs and fruits, in the bottom of a mixing glass prior to adding the liquid ingredients. Examples would be mint and simple syrup or nectar, or lime with bitters and sugar. The point is not to mash everything together, but to release the herb's essence or the fruit's juice into the sweetener, and typically 2–3 firm turns of the muddler will do the job perfectly.

Building: Building is simply pouring one liquid onto another, and in most cases (see floating for the exception), it is not essential what order this is done in. Many of your tall mixed drinks are built directly in the glass by pouring the ingredients over ice.

Rolling: The technique of rolling is fun for tall drinks (see bloody maria recipe on page 58) as an alternative to stirring or shaking. Basically, you pour the ingredients into one tall glass (or half of a Boston shaker), hold it in one hand, and hold an empty, similarly sized glass in the other hand. Pour the drink back and forth between the two vessels a few times to mix everything together. If you get good at this, you can increase the distance between glasses and make a show of your technique, hopefully without spilling.

Floating: To float is to create layers of ingredients in a glass. There is a science behind what can be layered on top of another ingredient, and it is based on the specific gravity of the liquid: heavy liquids sink, light liquids rise. If a recipe calls for floating or a float, use your bar spoon and slowly pour the top-layer liquid over the back of the bar spoon. Avoid big splashes, and don't stir or the effect will be lost.

Rimming a glass: One of the popular options when serving a margarita is to add a salted rim. This is an easy technique to master. Salts, sugars, and other granular ingredients can be used.

To rim a glass, begin by wetting the rim with a liquid that complements the drink. For many, this will be a piece of lemon, lime, orange, or whatever fruit you may have cut for a garnish. Use the excess fruit and run the pulp around the rim of the glass. Then roll the outside of the rim in a plate filled with salt (kosher salt is preferred for rimming) or sugar. The goal is to create a thin, even layer on the outside of the rim, without any clumps. Gently tap any excess off the glass over the sink.

Rimming Alternatives

There are many ways to customize the rim of a glass. Colored sugars that are commonly used in baking can be combined to fit any occasion. Cocoa is great for sweet drinks, like a chocolate margarita. Combine salt and cracked pepper or chili powder for a little spice; think of combining sugar with ground cinnamon, nutmeg, or ginger for winter drinks; or use crushed bacon bits on drinks that are a bit more savory. In some instances the citrus base may not be appropriate or ideal, and a liqueur — like one used in the cocktail — can be used to wet the rim instead (for example, an amaretto and cocoa rim, a ginger liqueur and cinnamon sugar rim, or a limoncello and sugar rim).

Agave Nectar, Simple Syrup & Infusions

Agave Nectar

Agave nectar is a natural choice for sweetening tequila cocktails. Also called agave syrup, it is made from the same juices of the agave plant that are fermented and distilled to make tequila. When the extracted juices are heated slowly, the carbohydrates break down into a (nonalcoholic) sugary syrup called agave nectar.

The nectar is available in a variety of grades and colors. The lightest are most similar to simple syrup and the darker grades are sweeter, with a more intense agave flavor. Look for agave nectars that are made of 100% blue agave and are labeled with a "Certificate of Origin" or as a "Product of Mexico." Many are certified organic and can be found at large supermarkets and natural food stores.

Because agave nectar has a lower glycemic index than other sweeteners, many people use it as a substitute for sugars in food and drink. It is now a common replacement for simple syrup and can be used in any cocktail. Still, agave nectar is sweeter than simple syrup, so when making this substitution, cut the amount by a quarter to half of what is recommended for the simple syrup.

Simple Syrup

There are instances when agave nectar is not useful, and good, old-fashioned simple syrup is the better option. The most likely case for this is when you want to infuse simple syrup with a certain flavor. It is easier to infuse simple syrup while making it than to attempt to infuse preproduced agave nectar.

To infuse simple syrup, begin with the *simple syrup* recipe of equal parts sugar and distilled water (for a richer syrup, use 2 parts sugar to 1 part water), with the flavoring agent in a pan. Bring this to a boil, stirring constantly until the sugar is completely dissolved. Remove from heat and allow the syrup to cool completely. Strain it through a fine strainer until all of the herb, botanical, or fruit particles are removed, then bottle and store it in the refrigerator.

Syrup Flavors

Fresh or dried herbs and botanicals, food-grade essential oils and water essences, and fresh fruits can be used to add flavor to simple syrup. Use the whole leaves of herbs like mint, rosemary, and lavender, and cut vanilla beans, fruits, and the like into ¼-inch slices. Check the labels of oils and flavored waters to ensure they are consumable. Rose essence or orange-flower water can be used as a portion of the unflavored water of the syrup. A good starting point for this is 1:1, which can be adjusted to taste.

Tequila Infusions

Tequila infusions appear regularly in the recipes of this book, for the simple fact that an infusion is an easy way to enhance any drink with a subtle flavor, and tequila just happens to be a perfect candidate for this.

To infuse any distilled spirit, begin with your choice of flavor, determine how to extract that into the liquor, combine the two, and wait. It may not be quite that simple, but that is the basic formula.

Infusing flavors into liquor is not an exact science. It is best to put together an infusion, check it after a few days, and if needed, continue infusing until it is perfect. This is especially important when working with strong, pungent flavors such as hot peppers, and in these cases it is recommended to infuse, not for days, but for hours at a time. Where it may take five to seven days to obtain an aromatic, beautiful herbal infusion, a jalapeño, habanero, or other pepper is usually best within the first couple of hours.

Below is a very general guide to infusion times:

- **1–2 hours**: Hot peppers, horseradish, and other generally pungent flavors.

- **3–4 days**: Intensely flavored herbs and fruits such as vanilla bean, lemon, orange, grapefruit, lime, mint, garlic, tarragon, basil, oregano, dill, thyme, and bell pepper.

- **1 week**: Moderately flavored fruits like cantaloupe, strawberry, peach, mango, tangerine, cherry, and berry.

- **2 weeks**: Mild flavors such as pineapple, ginger, and lemongrass.

Fresh herbs can be placed in the liquor whole; simply cut sprigs and add them to the infusion. Dried herbs will require longer infusions. Fruits and vegetables should be sliced or diced, and in most cases the peel can remain; exceptions would be melon, pineapple, and other hard-skinned produce. Berries can be left whole, though it is best to score the skins of harder varieties. Peppers can be added either whole, scored, or sliced, in which case it is best to remove the seeds.

To make your infusion, begin with a clean glass container that has a tight lid. Tall mason jars and empty (cleaned) liquor bottles are two nice options, though the wider the mouth, the easier it is to add the flavoring agent. Pour tequila (blanco is recommended) into the container and add the herb, fruit, or vegetable. Secure the lid and give the jar a few hearty shakes. Store this infusion in a cool, dark place and give a shake several times a day. After a few days, take a small taste to sample the flavor and decide whether it is intense enough or should stay in a day or two longer. When the infusion has reached its peak of flavor, use a fine strainer, cheesecloth, or paper coffee filter to remove all of the flavoring ingredient. Repeat the straining until you are left with only liquid (depending on how fine the particles are, multiple passes through a strainer may be required).

Blending Tips

It rarely fails that you can grab someone's attention with the whir of a blender. That distinct noise is like a calling card that a fantastic, super-cold drink is on its way. On a hot day, there are few things that are more satisfying. The process of making frozen drinks is fun and another instance where you can let your imagination run wild.

Here are a few tips for getting the most out of your blender:

- Test your blender's ice-chopping skills with ice alone to find the perfect speeds for the desired effect. Begin on slow speeds and work your way up to have more control over the consistency.

- Add the ingredients, *then* the ice, to ensure that everything is mixed and chopped completely before the majority of the ice chopping begins.

- It takes about one cup of ice to make one drink. Add more ice to make the drink thicker or a little more of one of the liquids to thin it.

- To avoid a mess, double-check that the pitcher is seated on the base and the lid is secure before turning on the blender.

- Clean your blender after each use, especially when switching flavors or making nonalcoholic drinks after a round of cocktails.

Glassware

The glasses used for tequila cocktails are of the standard variety. For the majority of drinks, you will use a cocktail (martini) glass, a lowball or old-fashioned glass, a tall highball or collins glass, or a shot glass. The style, size, and sometimes even the shape of individual glassware within each of those categories will vary greatly and can be fun to collect.

Margaritas have their own glassware options. They are often served straight in a cocktail glass, frozen in the classic-styled margarita glass, on the rocks in either of those, in a lowball, or in a stemmed bowl-shaped glass.

The tall, skinny shot glasses that are commonly used for tequila shots and sangrita are called caballitos ("small horses"). These single-sip glasses were thought of as the "official" tequila glass and derive from the small ox horns, or *cuernitos*, that Mexican horsemen drank their tequila from while on the trail.

A classic margarita served "neat" with a lime wedge

CHAPTER 3:

Tequila Drinks

■ ■ ■ ■ ■ ■ ■ ■ ■ ■ ■ ■

Cocktails

Tequila is a natural cocktail ingredient. It has a flavor profile unlike any other distilled spirit and can be paired with almost as many flavors as the "tasteless" vodka. Unlike vodka, tequila's earthy, vegetal qualities create a unique background for cocktails that tends to bring the drinks down to earth. Layering flavors on top of tequila is interesting to play around with.

Though tequila may be versatile, it does have a few "natural" flavor pairings. You can rely on citrus (namely lemon, lime, orange, and grapefruit), chocolate, coffee, and hot peppers to complement tequila in almost every instance. Examples of these can be found in many of the great tequila cocktails. Many of these flavors are natural because they can also be found in Mexican cuisine and have an indigenous and symbiotic relationship with the Mexican liquor. Start with these flavors, find what you enjoy, and explore from there.

There are very few common and unique cocktail ingredients that do not work in tequila's favor. From the sweet to the tart, the spicy to the herbaceous, finding flavors that contradict tequila is extremely rare. When a flavor combination seems a little off, usually a small adjustment can be made to make it work. That may mean working out the ratio of ingredients or adding an ingredient that binds the contradictions together.

Luckily there is a growing consensus among modern mixologists and tequila aficionados that tequila is versatile, and the result has been the development of some fantastic new drinks. It feels like every time you turn around, some creative soul has found a new match for the taste of tequila. Rarely are these discoveries disappointing.

My hope is that the following recipes inspire you to take a fresh look at tequila — both figuratively and literally — and how it is used in cocktails. With luck this may jump-start your own creativity, so more fascinating cocktails can be developed.

I have included some of the tried-and-true tequila cocktails that will always hold a place in the cocktail world. I've also expanded on those to show the inspiration that can come from each recipe. It is amazing how a single flavor can transform a drink into something wholly different. The other drinks are from my personal experience with this ambidextrous liquor. My main goal with each recipe is to make it attainable by everyone. Rarely will you find an ingredient included that is so exotic or far-fetched that it cannot be found locally or at least be ordered. I agree with the theory that real people want real drinks that they can make without going to the ends of the Earth to find the ingredients. From there it is merely a matter of combining the ordinary to make something extraordinary, and that is what the cocktail is all about.

Margarita

The margarita is without a doubt the most popular tequila cocktail. It has been adapted more times than can be counted and has a rich, though debated, history. For as many variations as this cocktail has, this shaken lime version started it all.

The best margaritas use a premium, usually blanco, tequila and fresh-squeezed lime juice. When it comes to triple sec, you will find many available. Cointreau is popularly considered the premium choice for this orange liqueur (see sidebar on orange liqueurs on page 25), and though Grand Marnier is sometimes used, its brandy base does not lend as well to the margarita.

- 1½ fl. oz. blanco tequila
- 1 fl. oz. triple sec or other orange liqueur
- ¾ fl. oz. fresh lime juice

Combine the ingredients in a cocktail shaker filled with ice, shake well, and strain into a chilled margarita or cocktail glass.
Garnish: lime wedge, maraschino cherry, and lemon peel

Tips
- Fill the glass with ice prior to straining to serve the drink "on the rocks."

- Rim the glass by wetting the edge with a lime wedge and dipping it into salt (see pages 29–30 for tips).

- Use 1 cup of ice and add the ingredients to a blender for a frozen margarita (see strawberry margarita on page 42 for more suggestions).

- For a slightly sweeter drink, add a dash of simple syrup.

Variations:
1. Create a **blue margarita** by using blue curaçao in place of the triple sec. Both are orange liqueurs, so the flavor will not change, just the color.

2. Experiment with flavor-infused tequilas. Flavors you may want to try include strawberry, kiwi, and jalapeño.

3. Upgrade the margarita by switching to higher-quality liquors. Try premium reposado tequila and the brandy-based orange liqueur Grand Marnier to create a **cadillac margarita**.

4. Another popular variation of the cadillac margarita is the **highland margarita**, which adds ½ fl. oz. of Drambuie, a Scotch-based liqueur.

Blue curaçao margarita

The Story of the Margarita

In the last few decades of the 20th century, the margarita owned the cocktail scene. This was the drink that almost everyone gravitated toward and, besides shots of straight tequila, was practically the only way drinkers got a taste of tequila. It was during this time that creative bartenders began to adapt the popular drink to include almost any flavor one could think of. Cocktail menus continue to be littered with these flavor options, alongside a variety of margaritas that call for one particular brand (usually top-shelf) or another of tequila.

Though the margarita had its heyday in the 1980s and '90s, it has roots dating back to the beginning of the century. We are not sure exactly when it was created and who was behind it. There are almost as many claims to the birth of the margarita as there are varieties of the cocktail; a few of those are acceptable and are feasible, though we will never know which was first or if any or all are simply one of those rather inventive bar tales that are so common. It is also possible that there may have been multiple people in multiple places who created the mix of tequila, lime, and triple sec without knowing that other bartenders were doing the same. This is a frequent occurrence, even today.

I tend to go along with that theory, based on the fact that the margarita

thoughts on margarita mix

Bottled margarita mixes are an interesting subject. Some contain tequila, making them a "margarita in a bottle," and many do not. At times it is hard to tell whether a particular mix does or does not, and many consumers either find themselves reading what seems to be a novel's worth of label language to find out, or they realize one or two drinks in that they are merely consuming sugar water and no tequila. What they are getting instead is often neon-colored syrup that is filled with all sorts of unpronounceable and unnatural additives and has an abnormal aftertaste.

Why choose a margarita mix? I cannot justify buying or recommending a bottled margarita mix on most occasions for one simple reason: a margarita is far too easy to make. How can you cut corners on a drink that essentially contains four ingredients: tequila, lime juice, triple sec, and ice? With the nonalcoholic mixes, you still need two of those four ingredients to make a drink — the tequila and ice — and many of us already have either limes or lime juice and an orange liqueur in our bars and kitchens. This contradicts the margarita mixes' marketing premise that they are convenient. Your made-from-scratch margarita is going to be superior in taste and takes maybe a minute longer to make than one from a mix, which, by the way, you also need to shake, stir, or blend.

Fresh is where it's at when it comes to the margarita.

is a very basic sour drink, similar to other cocktails of the time. In his book *Imbibe! From Absinthe Cocktail to Whiskey Smash, a Salute in Stories and Drinks to "Professor" Jerry Thomas, Pioneer of the American Bar*, David Wondrich points out that the margarita may have been derived from the popular "daisy" drinks of the time. The brandy daisy was a hit in the 1800s ,and its mix of brandy, curaçao (orange liqueur), simple syrup, and lemon seems very familiar when looking at the margarita. Considering gin, rum, and whiskey were also mixed into daisies, it is likely that tequila followed suit. Also, the Spanish translation of daisy is *margarita*, so this theory is very plausible.

Margarita Claims

Who actually created the margarita? No one knows for sure. In fact, most of the common stories have contradictory facts within themselves. So, with all this mystery, the best thing to do is enjoy the stories and say "¡Salud!" to whomever that wonderful person was — you know the truth and the rest of us will just keep guessing.

Here are a few of the claims to fame:

- San Antonio (or was it Dallas?) socialite Margarita Sames created it in 1948 at her Acapulco vacation home, during a party for one of the Hiltons of hotel fame. Sames made a big deal of her claim and toured the United States for Cointreau, making sure everyone knew her version of events.

- Daniel "Danny" Negrete made this drink for his salt-loving girlfriend Margarita (or was her name Marjorie?) in 1936 while working at the Garci Crespo Hotel in Puebla, Mexico.

- Doña Bertha, owner of Bertha's Bar in Taxco, Mexico, had a drink named after her sometime in the 1930s. This recipe of tequila, lime, sugar, and orange bitters appears in the 1946 *The Gentleman's Companion, Volume I* (Charles H. Baker Jr.). Bertha's second drink, which used orange liqueur and skipped the bitters, was called the margarita.

- Los Angeles bartender Johnny Durlesser is reported to have created the drink in the 1950s at Tail of the Cock. José Cuervo distributor Vern Underwood made the claim and used the margarita in an exorbitant advertising campaign.

- In 1948, at the Rancho La Gloria near Tijuana, it is said that Carlos "Danny" Herrera made the cocktail for actress Marjorie King, who went by the name (you guessed it) Margarita when in Mexico.

- Francisco "Pancho" Morales may have made the first margarita on the Fourth of July while working at Tommy's Place in Juarez, Mexico.

- Don Carlos Orozco made the drink for a German ambassador's daughter, Margarita Henkel, one slow afternoon at Hussong's Cantina in Ensenada, Mexico, in 1941.

Clockwise: blue margarita, classic lime margarita, frozen strawberry margarita

Strawberry Margarita

Strawberries naturally evoke thoughts of the frozen drink. Think of not only the margarita, but the frozen daiquiri, the strawberry smoothie, and the host of other blended goodies that include strawberries. This is why the strawberry margarita remains the most popular frozen margarita and is worth revisiting.

The base recipe is simple: tequila, strawberries, orange liqueur, and lime. Blend it all up with ice and there you have it. Simple, right? It may seem simple, and it really is, but I have seen so many strawberry margaritas go wrong.

How do you make a spectacular strawberry margarita? Begin with fresh! Fresh strawberries always make the better drink, especially when they are in season and can be picked right off the vine. Packaged frozen strawberries are a last resort, and if this drink is a year-round indulgence, you may want to think about freezing your own. The next degradation would be to use a strawberry liqueur, which some recipes do, but that only defeats the purpose of a refreshing, fruity cocktail. Considering the lime, it is only logical that if you have fresh limes around for garnishing, you can spare some for juice and improve your drink just that much more.

The second factor to making this cocktail superior is in the choice of alcohol. You do not have to employ your top-shelf tequila here, but a moderately priced blanco is going to make a world of difference over the bottom-shelf gold tequila.

- *1½ fl. oz. blanco tequila*
- *1 fl. oz. Cointreau*
- *1 fl. oz. fresh-squeezed lime juice*
- *½ cup sliced fresh strawberries*

Combine the ingredients in a blender and puree until well mixed. Add 1 cup of ice and blend until smooth. Pour into a frozen margarita glass.

Garnish: strawberry

Tips

- Begin with strawberries that are sliced, and then blend them into the consistency of a puree before adding ice, to ensure the smoothest drink.

- Play with the strawberry garnish: cut a slice into a whole fruit and rest it on the glass rim, or cut a fruit into thin slices to be fanned on top of the drink, or dip the fruit in melted chocolate and lay it on the drink.

- A frozen glass is key to keeping your margarita from becoming soupy too quickly. Place glasses in the freezer or upside down in an ice bucket until they are nice and frosty.

Variations:

1. Switch out the fruit or add multiple fresh fruits according to the season. Almost any fruit will work in a margarita, especially pomegranate, watermelon, banana, tangerine, and peach.

2. Layer your frozen margaritas. Blend a batch of one flavor and store it in the refrigerator (the freezer is often too cold if you work slowly) while blending up another fruit blend. Pour one on top of the other in the glass.

3. The popular **Hawaiian margarita** is made with fresh strawberries and pineapple, but an even more interesting variation of this tropical delight is tangerine and pineapple.

Jalapeño Margarita

Tequila and hot peppers go together like peanut butter and jelly. The pair has an inherent relationship that is truly wonderful when handled properly, and no other liquor can handle spicy as well as tequila does. It is a natural fit, given the two ingredients' Mexican roots, and this is the reason you will find so many spicy tequila cocktails.

This jalapeño margarita is a fine example of this marriage. The recipe as it is given is not too spicy, but just spicy enough to remind you that there is a jalapeño involved. Between the liquor, nectar, and citrus, there is enough sweet and tart for a well-balanced drink.

There is a reason behind the liquor choices made in this margarita. The reposado tequila's slightly sweet oakiness simultaneously enhances and mellows the pepper's heat. There is something to be said about the reposado's value as the middle ground of tequila, and a drink like this is a fine example of using it for both the more natural agave flavor and the gentle aging.

Grand Marnier (or another brandy-based orange liqueur) also has a dual role. It adds a rich texture and just enough orange flavor to complement the pepper. Lighter orange liqueurs like triple sec and curaçao are too bitter in this instance.

- 4 slices jalapeño pepper, seeded
- ¼ fl. oz. agave nectar
- 1 ½ fl. oz. reposado tequila
- ¾ fl. oz. Grand Marnier
- ¾ fl. oz. fresh-squeezed lime juice
- 2 dashes orange bitters

Muddle (see p. 29 for instructions) the pepper and nectar in the bottom of a cocktail shaker. Add the other ingredients and ice and shake vigorously. Strain the mix once into a spare glass and a second time into a well-chilled cocktail glass.
Garnish: whole jalapeño or a slice

Tips

- It is best to double-strain this drink in order to remove any pepper particles. An alternative would be to pour the drink through a fine strainer into the serving glass.

- By removing the pepper seeds, you get a milder drink. The seeds contain most of the jalapeño's heat and are nearly impossible to completely strain out. The easiest way to remove seeds from a slice of pepper, along with the core, is to use a vegetable peeler.

Variations:

1. Make this cocktail into an international affair by creating a spicy **sake-rita**. Muddle the jalapeño and nectar, then add 1 fl. oz. each blanco tequila and sake and ½ fl. oz. each lime juice and either lychee or curaçao liqueur. Shake, double-strain, and add orange bitters.

2. A **savory chile margarita** can be made by blending 1½ fl. oz. reposado tequila, ½ fl. oz. each pineapple and tomato juices and chile pepper puree, and a couple of dashes of both fresh lemon juice and hot sauce with 1 cup of ice. Garnish with a bit of cracked pepper on top.

3. For a truly unique margarita, make a **guacarita**. Blend 1½ fl. oz. blanco tequila, ½ fl. oz. each lime juice and triple sec, and 1 cup of ice with a quarter of a skinned avocado and 6 cilantro leaves.

Chocolate Margarita

When dessert and drink come together, the result is paradise. The chocolate margarita and the other sweet drinks here are designed to do just that: indulge both your sweet tooth and love for fine cocktails in one fell swoop.

Tequila and chocolate are yet another divine flavor combination, though it can be difficult to get the two to join in a happy marriage. Often we will see chocolate in lighter tequila cocktails — maybe a chocolate liqueur used as an accent to other flavors, or a drizzle of syrup as a fancy garnish (see melon cocoa drizzle on page 84), or a few dashes of chocolate bitters in the style of Mexican mole sauce. When it comes to an indulgently decadent chocolate cocktail, this chocolate margarita is about as chocolaty as it gets. This is one of a handful of dessert drinks that tequila actually works rather well in.

The chocolate liqueur used here is open to interpretation. There are some wonderful chocolate liqueurs available. Many of the more "boutique" brands come and go from the market but are worthy of picking up when they cross your path. An option that is always available is crème de cacao, which is available in either brown or white. For this drink, I do recommend the brown variety for aesthetics.

You will note that a little citrus is added in the recipe. This helps bind the sweetness of the chocolate to the tequila and adds depth to the drink's flavor, making it more interesting than a tequila-flavored chocolate smoothie.

- 2 fl. oz. blanco tequila
- 1 fl. oz. chocolate liqueur
- 1 fl. oz. cream or half-and-half
- Splash of fresh orange juice
- Splash of fresh lime juice
- Dash chocolate bitters

Place the ingredients in a blender and mix well, then add 1 cup of ice and blend until smooth. Pour into a margarita glass that has been rimmed with a mix of sugar and cocoa.
Garnish: sugar and cocoa for rimming

Tips
- Experiment with the garnish on this drink. Suggestions include dark chocolate shavings sprinkled on top or swirling lines of chocolate syrup inside a frozen glass.
- Want more chocolate? Add chocolate syrup to the blender.
- Ensure that in this drink in particular, your ice is blended very well until the drink is very smooth. Chunky ice may be okay with fruits but is not so appetizing when chocolate is involved.

Variations:

1. A **choco-café margarita** is made by adding ½ fl. oz. coffee liqueur and using only ½ fl. oz. of cream in the recipe opposite.

2. Create a **coco margarita** by blending 2 fl. oz. tequila and 1 fl. oz. each of pineapple juice, crème de cacao, and cream of coconut with 1 cup of ice.

3. When apples are in season, use them in a similar frozen dessert drink. The **caramel apple margarita** is made by blending 2 fl. oz. tequila, 1 fl. oz. butterscotch schnapps, and 1½ fl. oz. orchard-fresh apple cider with 1 cup of ice. Garnish with a caramel-dipped apple slice.

Tamarind Margarita

The first time I tried the tamarind margarita, I was visiting Sauza Tequila Distillery in Tequila, Mexico. I could not think of a more appropriate occasion or setting to experience this cocktail. From that initial sip, I have been infatuated with this unique-tasting margarita.

What is so great about the tamarind margarita? For a native Midwesterner, it is probably the exotic flavor of the tamarind that captured my fancy. I just didn't get that as a kid. Though I have known of tamarind for years and tasted it in a variety of international foods, tamarind paired with tequila in a beverage is a brand-new experience.

The tamarind, though native to Africa, is quite popular in Mexican cuisine and is grown throughout Mexico. The flavor is very distinct acidic tart with a tropical sweetness. The most common (and easiest) way to use it in cocktails is to buy the packaged paste, also called tamarind concentrate.

- 2 fl. oz. *blanco tequila*
- ½ fl. oz. *Cointreau*
- ¾ oz. *tamarind paste*
- ½ fl. oz. *fresh-squeezed lemon juice*
- ½ fl. oz. *agave nectar*

Add the ingredients with 1 cup of ice to a blender and blend until completely smooth. Pour into a margarita or collins glass with a chili powder and sugar rim. Garnish: chili powder and sugar for rimming

Tips

- Mix the rimming ingredients together in a flat tray until the two colors become one.

- The chili powder/sugar rim may not be for everyone. Other options include ground cinnamon or nutmeg with sugar or Tajín Fruit Seasoning.

Variations:

1. Try a **yuzu margarita** by using yuzu juice or a puree of the yuzu fruit instead of tamarind. This little citrus is used in Asian cuisine, and the peel makes a great cocktail garnish.

2. Make a **lychee margarita** (see el tigre shooter for more on lychee on page 102) by using 1 fl. oz. lychee liqueur or juice in place of tamarind. If desired, spice can be added with either a dash of wasabi or chili powder.

3. Orange-flavored margaritas are okay, but I would recommend using blood oranges. This fruit is darker than Florida oranges and contains less acid, for a richer flavor. Its perfect for tequila cocktails, and its juice can be used in this recipe as a substitute for tamarind.

Margarita de Madagascar

Another exotic margarita, the margarita de Madagascar is fascinating because of its many layers of flavor. Its primary flavor is vanilla, which is as native to Mexico as the agave plant, making it a natural pairing for tequila and hot peppers. Today, much of the vanilla we use is a variety grown halfway around the world in Madagascar.

In this cocktail I use two forms of vanilla, the tiny beans and a delicious vanilla liqueur called Navan. The mellow flavors of vanilla are delightful and tame the spicy qualities of both the tequila and pepper. You may be familiar with the long, nearly black vanilla bean pod and may have used it to infuse liquor. In this instance, I am more interested in the vanilla beans enveloped in the pod. They are where the real flavor comes from. That is why we slice the pod, remove the tiny black beans, and muddle them with jalapeño and agave nectar.

- ½ vanilla bean pod, seeded
- 3 slices jalapeño pepper
- ¼ fl. oz. agave nectar
- 1½ fl. oz. reposado tequila
- 1 fl. oz. Navan vanilla liqueur
- Juice of ½ lime

In the bottom of a cocktail shaker, muddle the small vanilla beans, jalapeño slices, and agave nectar. Add ice and the other ingredients and shake vigorously. Strain into a cocktail glass.

Garnish: vanilla bean pod

Tips

- Slice the vanilla bean pod lengthwise and scrape the beans into the cocktail shaker using a knife.

- Remember to remove the core and seeds from the pepper.

- Whole vanilla bean pods are expensive, so you may skip the garnish. If you do opt for the garnish, simply lay a long section of the pod across the top of the glass or hook it on the rim and allow it to float in the drink.

Variations:

1. Make a **vanilla melon margarita** by skipping the pepper and using ½ fl. oz. each vanilla and melon liqueurs.

2. Try a **ginger rose margarita**. Infuse the tequila with rosemary, and use ½ fl. oz. each vanilla and ginger liqueurs. Again, skip the pepper.

3. Try fruit infusions in the tequila. Good choices include melon, apple, papaya, and strawberry.

Paloma

The paloma is the first drink every tequila initiate should have, and yet it often remains in the shadows. Maybe it does not have the potential for flair that the margarita has. Maybe its streamlined recipe has the connotation of plainness. Maybe it is because grapefruit soda is not as procurable as it should be. Whatever the reason, outside of Mexico the paloma is sadly under-appreciated.

The paloma is a lovely drink that has captured the hearts of Mexicans for years and combines their proclivity for its three simple ingredients: tequila, lime, and grapefruit soda. The endearment of the drink is also apparent in its name, as *paloma* translates into English as "dove," a name fitting this gentle drink.

The popular brand of grapefruit soda in Mexico is Jarritos. Squirt is another widely available option, and a number of other zingy grapefruit sodas continue to pop up. Other citrus sodas do make a suitable substitute, though to make a paloma what it is, grapefruit should be included. In this instance, or if using club soda, add 2 ounces of grapefruit juice for a drink that is dubbed *la paloma suprema*.

- *2 fl. oz. blanco or reposado tequila*
- *½ fl. oz. fresh lime juice*
- *Grapefruit soda*

Pour the tequila and lime juice into a collins or other tall glass filled with ice. Top with grapefruit soda.
Garnish: lime wheel

Variations:

1. The **cantarito** (see photo opposite, tall glass) is also one of those hidden tequila greats. Add 1 fl. oz. each fresh lemon and orange juice to the paloma recipe.

2. Use lavender-infused tequila to create a **lavenda paloma**. Other infusion options include lemongrass, pepper, vanilla, pear, and berry.

3. Thyme for a paloma? Make one by muddling thyme and 2 lime wedges. Add the tequila, ice, and grapefruit soda as above. Enjoy the play on words while serving.

Tequila Sour

Sours are a classic family of drinks, and tequila has naturally been integrated into the lineup. You may notice a similarity between the tequila sour and the classic margarita and you would be correct, because the margarita is, in a broad sense, classified as a sour. Save the absence of orange liqueur, the preference of lemon over lime, and the addition of a sweetener, the tequila sour is similar to its more famous counterpart. Therefore, if you enjoy one, it is likely you will like the other.

Classic sours are dominated by whiskey and have been a hit among drinkers since the middle of the 19th century. Tequila's home in this category is a relatively new development. Its sours recipe has been adapted to fit this particular base liquor. This recipe is my interpretation and leaves room for further adaptation based on personal taste.

The most prominent note in this recipe is that I split the lemon with lime juice. Most sours rely solely on lemon for the "sour," but as many tequila drinks have proven, lime is a natural complement to tequila and, in this instance, binds it to the lemon.

The tequila sour is a *perfect* drink to use the tequila of your choice. Whether that is a blanco, reposado, or an añejo, the sweet and sour enhances each in a unique way, and the one you choose will be a matter of personal preference.

- 1 ½ fl. oz. tequila
- ¾ fl. oz. fresh-squeezed lemon juice
- ¾ fl. oz. fresh-squeezed lime juice
- ½ fl. oz. simple syrup

Shake the ingredients in a cocktail shaker filled with ice. Strain into a sour glass or small cocktail glass.
Garnish: lemon wheel or twist

Tips
- Traditionally, sours were served over ice. Modern interpretations tend to serve them neat. Either is a nice option, though if ice is used, switch to an old-fashioned glass.
- Make and store a fresh sour mix for use in this and other cocktails. Do this by adding ½ cup each lemon and lime juices to 1 cup simple syrup. Store in the refrigerator and simply shake it with tequila for your next tequila sour.

Variations:

1. Make a **limón melón sour** by beginning with lemon balm–infused tequila and adding ½ fl. oz. melon liqueur to the opposite.

2. Get exotic with a **guava sour.** Infuse the simple syrup with kaffir lime leaf and add ½ fl. oz. guava puree or juice to the recipe.

3. One of the classic renditions of the whiskey sour was to add a red wine (referred to as claret) float. Do this with the tequila sour as well for a traditional twist.

Tequini

The classic gin martini has been adapted so many times that the variations, including many that resemble it in glassware and name alone, are hard to keep an accurate count of. There are a few, however, that celebrate the progenitor in moderate ways. The tequini, or tequila martini, is one of those, and calls for a simple substitution of tequila for gin.

As similar as the two drinks are, it is obvious that the flavor is entirely different. Here we trade a blend of botanicals for sweet agave; while both are "earthy" in a sense, they are polar opposites.

I like to include the tequini in martini drink menus and use it often. The menu typically includes a stock of gin, vodka, whiskey, and tequila, with both sweet and dry vermouth and a variety of bitters. With this small bar stock I can affordably offer guests a range of neat drinks to sample — from the gin or vodka martini to a manhattan or a tequini. Each is available in either a dry, sweet, or perfect (sweet and dry, 1:1) style.

The choice of tequila is essential when making a tequini, because there is not much else in the drink that will disguise low-quality tequila. Typically, I prefer a premium blanco with dry vermouth, though reposados (especially from Jalisco's highlands) are highly recommended as well. When it comes to the Spanish Harlem, I do not hesitate to pull out my best añejo on hand. The tequini is one of the best drinks to show off your top-shelf tequilas, so do it.

- *2 fl. oz. blanco tequila*
- *½ fl. oz. dry vermouth*
- *2 dashes aromatic bitters*

Combine the ingredients in an ice-filled cocktail shaker. Stir for 30 seconds. Strain into a chilled cocktail glass.
Garnish: hot pepper or lime peel

Tips

- I follow the martini rule for shaking versus stirring. It is recommended that when alcohol is alone in the drink, it is best to stir. When juices, fruits, and other strong flavors are used, go ahead and shake it up.

- Because the tequini is so "clean," the garnish is open to interpretation. A lime peel or wedge gives the option of adding a touch of citrus, and peppers bring in a little flair. I've tried olives but feel they are best left to gin.

- The companies that make bitters continually expand the flavors available. Tequini favorites include grapefruit, chocolate mole, celery, and orange.

Variations:

1. The **Spanish Harlem** is a common option that is essentially a sweet tequini. Switch to an aged tequila and sweet vermouth, using orange bitters and peel for accents.

2. For a spicy option, try a **habanero martini** by dropping a whole habanero pepper into the glass. It will slowly infuse the cocktail and will not be too spicy before you reach the bottom of the drink.

3. The tequini is an ideal base for herb-infused tequilas. Favorites include lavender, lemongrass, and basil.

Tequila Sunrise

One may think that there is not much to say about the tequila sunrise. I beg to differ. You may be surprised that this seemingly innocent drink has a storied past. The debates begin, as with so many cocktails, with the drink's origin.

Those stories agree on one thing — the tequila sunrise of yesterday is not how we know it today. It began not with orange juice or grenadine, but with crème de cassis, lime, and soda, with the one constant being the drink's "sunrise" effect. This is a sort of drinkable science experiment — the denser ingredients will sink to the bottom of the glass, slowly rise, and meld into the rest of the drink without mixing completely unless stirred.

The story continues. . . . The claim is made that in the early '70s, Bobby Lazoff and Billy Rice were bartending at the Trident Restaurant in Sausalito, California. To keep up with the tequila craze of the time, the duo began turning gin and vodka drinks into tequila cocktails. Some of these failed the conversion, but out of this a newly designed tequila sunrise was born, and it included orange juice. Over the years the soda was dropped and grenadine replaced the cassis, creating the sunrise of today.

New Tequila Sunrise

- 2 fl. oz. tequila
- 4 fl. oz. fresh-squeezed orange juice
- ½ fl. oz. grenadine

Pour the tequila into a collins glass filled with ice. Top with orange juice and then pour the grenadine into the drink — it will sink.
Garnish: orange slice and maraschino cherry

Original Tequila Sunrise

- 1½ fl. oz. tequila
- Juice of ½ lime
- Club soda
- ¾ fl. oz. crème de cassis

Pour the tequila and lime juice into a collins glass with ice. Top with soda water and pour the cassis into the drink — it will sink.
Garnish: lime wheel and maraschino cherry

Tequila Sunrising

The tequila sunrise has been used all over pop culture. Most notably, Mel Gibson, Kurt Russell, and Michelle Pfeiffer starred in a 1988 movie by the same name. In 1973, the Eagles released "Tequila Sunrise," which went to 64 on the Billboard Hot 100. Glenn Frey was drinking tequila at sunrise — not the cocktail — when he titled the song.

Tips

- Grenadine is made from pomegranate and can be made from scratch. Crème de cassis is made from French black currants.

- Do not stir the drink. Instead, serve it with a straw and let the drinker decide if and when to stir.

Variations:

1. Make a **frozen tequila sunrise** in the blender by mixing the orange juice and tequila with 1 cup of ice. Pour grenadine in the bottom of a margarita glass and top it with the blended mixture.

2. Switch the orange juice out for ruby red grapefruit juice for a **ruby red sunrise**.

3. Instead of sinking the sweetener, float one on top for a sunset effect. To do this, switch ingredients. Slowly pour blackberry brandy over the back of a bar spoon for a **tequila sunset**, or use Galliano for a **freddy fuddpucker** (the popular vodka version is a harvey wallbanger).

Bloody Maria

One of the ways I experiment with tequila in different flavor combinations is to use it as a substitute in cocktails that typically use vodka. With the main taste of the drink already established, it is interesting to see what role tequila plays. The bloody maria is a great example and one of my favorites. Vodka is not tasteless, but it doesn't have the raw-earth, vegetal taste that can only be found in tequila. The spicy tomato mix of the vodka-based bloody mary is a natural companion for tequila, especially for those who enjoy a little extra spice in their drinks. After discovering this, I have found myself missing the tequila taste in any other "bloody" drink.

Sometimes people use drinks like this to test their — or a friend's — ability to take the heat of the hot sauce and peppers; however, I like to add a caution about that. This is not a five-alarm burrito that comes with a tortilla, meat, and cheese to absorb some of the fire. This is a drink, and eating hot stuff is a completely different experience than drinking it. Even if you are not intending to show off your masculinity, or whatever your reasoning may be, remember that it is very easy to throw off the balance here, so it is best to take it easy with the hot elements. Begin with the recipe, taste it, and add more if you like.

- 2 fl. oz. tequila
- 1 tsp. horseradish
- 3 dashes Tabasco sauce
- 3 dashes Worcestershire sauce
- Squeeze of ½ lime
- 3 dashes celery salt
- 3 dashes black pepper
- Tomato juice

Combine the ingredients in a tall glass filled with ice. Stir very well or mix it by rolling (see Tip below) back and forth between two glasses. Add the garnish. Garnish: celery stalk and lemon slice

Tips

- Skip the horseradish if you like.

- Use your favorite hot sauce. Tabasco is commonly used, but specialty hot sauces like habanero, salsa verde, and garlic are perfect for this drink.

- "Rolling" is an interactive method used to mix drinks that have heavy ingredients. It does take some practice to get the technique down and be able to do it without spilling. I suggest giving it a try with ice and water at first. Use two similar-size glasses and begin with a short gap as you pour. As you get better, you can increase the gap and make it into a long-pour show for your guests.

Variations:

1. Make a **tini bloody maria** by muddling 3–4 cherry tomatoes in a cocktail shaker with the spices until you have a thin juice, adding 1½ fl. oz. tequila and ice, and shaking vigorously for about 30 seconds. Double-strain into a chilled tall glass and garnish by slitting another cherry tomato and resting it on the rim.

2. Add ½ teaspoon wasabi paste to the mix for a different style of heat.

3. Replace the tomato juice with clamato, add a dash of orange juice, and skip the horseradish. Mix this **reno maria** as above and add a sprinkling of nutmeg to the top.

El Diablo

El diablo, as the name suggests, is a devilish little drink, but it has a fascinating taste and can easily become a favorite of any tequila lover. It is a relaxing and sweet — not too sweet — drink. The reposado tequila and crème de cassis have a tempting, nectarous quality that lures you in. The lime kicks in a touch of tart, and the real antagonist here is the ginger beer.

If ginger ale were an angel, ginger beer would be a devil, so it is appropriately called for specifically in el diablo. Ginger beer brings out all the spice possible from ginger and, unlike its more gentle counterpart, it packs quite a punch. It tantalizes the taste buds and keeps you coming back for more. Because of this, you will often find it in drinks with a sweeter base like this, to rival the soda's intensity.

El diablo is a modern creation. Yet in its relatively short life span, it has acquired many well-deserved fans. It is delicious no matter how you take it.

- 1½ fl. oz. reposado tequila
- ½ fl. oz. crème de cassis
- ½ fl. oz. fresh-squeezed lime juice
- Ginger beer

In a cocktail shaker, combine tequila, cassis, and lime. Shake well and strain into a chilled, ice-filled old-fashioned glass. Top with ginger beer.
Garnish: lime wedge

Tips
- The density of crème de cassis makes it perfect for slowly integrating into the drink. Build the cocktail without it, then slowly pour it over a bar spoon and enjoy the show as it begins to mingle and spread.

- Stand two small lime wedges on the ice, pointing one end up on either side of the glass. This can look like devil horns and is a fun Halloween garnish.

Variations:
1. For a milder el diablo, substitute ginger ale for the ginger beer.

2. Using pomegranate liqueur in place of the cassis brightens up this drink's flavor profile.

3. Try something new by adding ½ fl. oz. ruby port and substituting either pomegranate liqueur or grenadine for the cassis.

Chimayó Cocktail

Another favorite of many tequila drinkers, the chimayó cocktail is an exceptional autumn drink when fresh apple cider is available.

It was the abundance of apples grown in the area around Chimayó, New Mexico, that inspired Arturo Jaramillo to create this drink in the 1960s. Jaramillo and his wife, Florence, converted the 19th-century family hacienda in Chimayó into a restaurant around that time, and he wanted a signature drink that utilized the valley's apples. The chimayó was born and remains the cocktail to order at Rancho de Chimayó.

The key to the chimayó is the apple cider, which should be unfiltered, fresh off the press. Filtered cider will do, but you will find the best chimayó is made with the pure, cloudy variety. Apples are available year-round, and it is not difficult to make your own cider (see Tips below). Yet, I enjoy the annual fall pilgrimage to local orchards to hand-pick the fruit in its prime and pick up a gallon of their freshest cider. Somehow, this makes the resulting chimayós more satisfying.

The rest of the chimayó is self-explanatory, and I enjoy switching between blanco and reposado tequilas. Crème de cassis makes another appearance here — a testament to its cohesiveness with tequila — and not only brings the drink together with its sweet smoothness, but gives the chimayó its signature pale purple/red hue.

- 1 ½ fl. oz. tequila
- 1 fl. oz. unfiltered apple cider
- ½ fl. oz. fresh lemon juice
- ¼ fl. oz. crème de cassis

Build the ingredients in an old-fashioned glass filled with ice. Stir well, garnish, and serve.
Garnish: apple slices

Tips

- To keep your apple garnish from yellowing, give it a quick dip in lemon juice and shake off any excess.

- Cut thin, unpeeled apple slices and wedges for the garnish. To add a touch of festive sweetness, dip them in caramel and allow them to dry.

- To make your own cider: Wash, core, and slice apples. Puree in a food processor and press through a cheesecloth to extract the juice. Store the cider in the refrigerator for up to a week.

Variations:

1. For a less sweet version, switch the cassis out for Benedictine or hazelnut liqueur, or do a 50/50 mix of either with the cassis.

2. Infuse the tequila with cinnamon and/or ginger for a little spice.

3. Build on the fruit flavors by adding ¼ fl. oz. plum wine.

Tangerine Burro

The moscow mule is a ginger beer drink most imbibers are familiar with. Along with the dark and stormy, it may be the only use some can think of for the spicy soda. To adapt the popular vodka, lime, and ginger beer mule into a tequila-based "burro," I have added tangerine. The easiest way to introduce the freshest possible taste of this citrus is by muddling.

Tangerines are seasonal in many parts of the world — typically available October through April in the Northern Hemisphere — so at times they can be difficult to find. In the off-season, mandarin oranges can be used, but I chose the tangerine here because it seems to work better at taming the spicy ginger. Yet another, and preferred, tangerine substitute would be a blood orange, specifically the Sanguinello variety from Sicily. Their season coincides almost exactly with the tangerine, though they can last into May. They tend to be sweeter, with a "bloody" red flesh that is always stunning in drinks.

As in el diablo, the same theory applies to the choice of tequila. Go with a sweeter reposado to balance out the ginger beer's strong personality. For an even greater contrast, go with an añejo.

- *2 slices tangerine, halved*
- *1 slice lime, halved*
- *½ fl. oz. agave nectar*
- *2 fl. oz. reposado tequila*
- *Ginger beer*

Muddle the fruits and nectar in an old-fashioned glass. Fill with cracked ice and add tequila. Top with ginger beer and stir well.
Garnish: tangerine twist

Tips

- Traditional English or Jamaican ginger beers are best and often have a delightful balance of sweet and spice.

- When muddling fruits like these, leave the peel intact for a cleaner look and press the juice out of the flesh with the muddler so they integrate into the nectar.

- Cut fruit slices in half for a better fit in the glass.

A woman selling fruit at the covered market in Guanajuato

Variations:

1. As fruits go in and out of season, add or substitute them into the mix. Pomelo and peach are two of my favorites.

2. Muddle savory herbs into the mix along with the citrus. Tarragon, oregano, and basil are all good options.

Cilantro-Cucumber Smash

There is something magical about relaxing on the patio, looking over the garden you just spent an afternoon toiling away in, with a drink in hand that comes right out of that very garden. This self-realized satisfaction is the inspiration for the cilantro-cucumber smash.

For years we have designed our gardens to not only fill our family's culinary needs, but our drink desires as well. I call it the Bartender's Garden, and in it vegetables, fruits, and herbs that create the freshest of cocktails can be found. This particular drink uses ingredients found in many gardens and has a delightful harvest-fresh feel.

- 5–6 torn cilantro leaves
- 2 (¼-inch) slices of cucumber, chopped
- ¼ fl. oz. agave nectar
- 1½ fl. oz. blanco tequila
- ½ fl. oz. St-Germain elderflower liqueur
- ¼ fl. oz. fresh-squeezed lime juice
- 2 dashes bitters

Muddle cilantro, cucumber, and nectar in the bottom of an old-fashioned glass, and then fill the glass with crushed ice. Add the liquors and juice to a cocktail shaker, fill with more crushed ice, and shake. Strain into the muddled old-fashion glass. Add two dashes of bitters.
Garnish: cucumber peel and sprig of cilantro

Tips

- It is easy to overpower the drink with too much cilantro, as it is a rather intense herb. Five to six medium-size leaves are just about perfect, though you can adjust to taste.

- I've found that I prefer vegetable or herbal bitters in this mix. The Bitter Truth makes a nice celery bitters, Fee Brothers also has a celery bitters, and Bar Keep Bitters Swedish Herb or Lavender Spice bitters are all nice options. However, when in doubt, that trusty bottle of aromatic bitters is pleasant.

- When muddling this mix, it is not necessary to mash the ingredients. The goal is to release the cilantro's oils into the nectar and cucumber. Crushed cucumber is a great flavor in this cocktail, but it is not too pretty in a glass, so go easy on it.

Variations:

1. Add pomegranate seeds to the muddled ingredients. The seeds will release their sweet juice, which is a surprisingly delightful complement to cucumber. Shake and strain.

2. Use avocado and ginger in place of the cucumber. A few cubes of ripe avocado and 2 thin slices of gingerroot add sweet and spicy flavors to the mix. Also, switch over to orange or aromatic bitters.

3. Begin with infused tequila. Hibiscus or ginger are okay in a reposado but those are not nearly as interesting as a jalapeno, or even horseradish, flavored blanco.

Piña de Picante

Pineapple, orange, and pepper are all natural complements to the persnickety flavor of tequila. In the piña de picante I have combined these four elements, and the result is a snappy, refreshing mixed drink with an unobtrusive kick.

When I developed the piña de picante, I did not want a strong pepper flavor, because too much spice is an undesirable contrast to these fruits, particularly the pineapple. Inspired by the in-glass infusion technique of the habanero martini (see Variations on page 55), I decided to employ the trick here. It works quite well, and I have found myself using it in a nonalcoholic version.

The subtle pepper flavor comes from allowing a pepper to rest in the drink. At first the spice is almost unnoticeable, but as we get further into the drink it grows in intensity while never getting too strong, even for the mildest of palates. Use a whole pepper, though it is best to score the pepper's flesh with a knife. I prefer to cut a spiral down the pepper and spread the connected sections apart before adding it to the drink. This allows the liquids to flow in and out of the pepper, picking up more spice from the interior and the seeds, where the majority of the spice is held. The spiciness of the piña de picante is going to depend on the pepper used. I prefer hot red peppers with a thick flesh for both flavor and visual aesthetics. Jalapeños are another nice option, though they are typically shorter and stouter than the longer, more elegant fresno and chile peppers.

- 2 fl. oz. tequila
- 4 fl. oz. fresh-squeezed orange juice
- 4 fl. oz. pineapple juice
- 1 whole red serrano pepper

Pour the tequila and juices into a highball glass filled with ice cubes. Stir well. Place a scored pepper into the drink, resting it amongst the ice, and allow it to infuse the drink with spice.

Tips

- Wash your hands thoroughly after handling hot peppers. This also gives more time for the infusion to begin.

- Serve the drink with a straw so it can be stirred as the pepper flavor evolves.

- This drink is best with fresh juices. Oranges can be squeezed by hand, but pineapple will require a juicer.

- If the drink begins to get too intense, remove the pepper.

Variations:

1. Add a floral note to the base by using hibiscus-infused tequila.

2. Sweeten the drink by adding ½ fl. oz. coconut milk.

3. Bring some sparkle into the mix by using 3 fl. oz. each orange and pineapple juices and topping the drink with mango soda or ginger ale.

Santa Maria

The santa maria is one of those cocktails that never really saw the limelight, and there is probably a good reason. The main issue I have with the original recipe is the spiced rum and gold tequila it calls for. Years of tasting premium spirits have produced a personal expectation that is often deflated by the use of lesser-quality rum and tequila. Despite that, combining rum and tequila in a martini-esque cocktail and upgrading the ingredients bring sophistication to the santa maria.

Switching to a smooth, premium light rum gives the santa maria a sweet, unadulterated base. The same argument applies to the cocktail's tequila. The maturity of a reposado is just the right touch needed. The only other adaptation is the addition of orange bitters.

- 1 ½ fl. oz. light rum
- 1 ½ fl. oz. reposado tequila
- ½ fl. oz. sweet vermouth
- 3 dashes orange bitters

Pour the ingredients into a cocktail shaker filled with ice. Stir well and strain into a chilled cocktail glass.
Garnish: orange wheel and maraschino cherry

Tips

- Make your own brandied or maraschino cherries for garnishing. To make, simply soak fresh cherries in either brandy or maraschino liqueur for a few days.

- Take advantage of the spiral on your bar spoon when stirring cocktails. Hold the spiral between your thumb and forefinger and spin it back and forth for 30 seconds. Whatever you do, do not stir a drink like it is a cake batter. Be gentle.

Variations:

1. Brighten up the drink by adding a splash of cranberry juice.

2. For a delicious autumn drink, try a **manzana santa maria** by infusing tequila with sliced apples and adding ¼ fl. oz. maraschino liqueur to the recipe.

3. For a drier, lighter version, a **santa maria de mango** is a nice option: 1½ fl. oz. mango-flavored rum, 1½ fl. oz. blanco tequila, ½ fl. oz. dry vermouth, a splash of fresh lemon juice, and orange bitters.

Passion Cocktail

The passion cocktail is, to put it simply, a tequila cosmopolitan. Once again, I upgrade from the gold tequila in the more common recipe to a blanco or reposado to mix with cranberry juice. Both the passion cocktail and the cosmopolitan were created during an era in which gold tequilas prevailed and, with the wider availability of the purer tequilas today, it would be a shame to forego such an upgrade.

Two schools of thought arose with this modern classic: one that makes a deep red, heavy-on-the-juice cosmopolitan, and the other that uses a splash of cranberry, creating a blushing pink drink, which is said to be how it was originally intended.

My preference, especially with tequila, is to go light. The heavier use of juice will hide the flavor of the spirit. When I adapt a vodka cocktail to a more flavorful spirit, I want to taste its characteristics, not lose them behind fruits. Also, the sweeter drinks tend to leave the body wanting more and more. It is a natural reaction with sugars, which is why it is easy to overindulge on desserts. When that physiological reaction happens with alcohol, the results can be harmful, and you can easily become more inebriated than you intended. The "drier" the drink, the more you taste its intoxicating contents.

- 1 ½ fl. oz. reposado tequila
- 1 fl. oz. Grand Marnier
- ½ fl. oz. fresh-squeezed lime juice
- ½ fl. oz. cranberry juice

Combine the ingredients in a cocktail shaker filled with ice. Shake well and strain into a chilled cocktail glass.
Garnish: lime wedge or peel

Variations:

1. Make a **strawberry passion** by substituting strawberry liqueur or juice for the cranberry.

2. Add a floral touch by using a lavender- or rosemary-infused tequila.

3. For an entirely different, more tart taste, use grapefruit juice in place of the cranberry and add a small splash of grenadine for color and sweetness.

Cerveza de Tequila

I mentioned in the "Types of Tequila" chapter that there have been a handful of "tequila-flavored" beers in the market from time to time. Though tequila is often not involved — agave nectar is used — the concept is a good one. Tequila and beer are great when combined, but I don't see the point in buying an imitation when the two are easily mixable, and the result is far superior.

Mexico is not only known for great tequilas, but a refreshing selection of beers as well. Many are exported now, and the list continues to grow. Mexican beers range from very light-bodied styles to dark ambers, the variety being influenced by the full scope of international brewers over the years. Personal preference will prevail when it comes to deciding which style to mix with tequila. I am fond of many in the spectrum, yet I gravitate toward the lighter brews in this case, as they allow you to thoroughly enjoy the tequila.

As delightful as tequila and beer may be collectively and individually, the cerveza de tequila needs another layer. Lime is a bit too obvious for my taste. Apricot nectar ended up being one of the best complements to both Mexican beverages, so I went with that.

- *2 fl. oz. blanco tequila*
- *½ fl. oz. apricot nectar*
- *Mexican beer*

Pour the tequila and apricot nectar into a pint glass and top with beer. Garnish: lime wedge and (optional) salt rim

Tips

- While the salt rim is optional according to taste, a lime garnish is highly recommended. The wedge, as opposed to a slice, holds more juice and gives the drinker the option to add as little or as much citrus as they want.

- I like to run my lime around the rim, then squeeze the juice into the drink before dropping it in.

Variations:

1. Get the taste of hops and mock the spiciness of a ginger beer by adding ½ fl. oz. ginger liqueur to the beer, tequila, and apricot nectar.

2. Alternatively, get a subtle ginger flavor by splitting the beer portion with a sweet ginger ale.

3. Create a **Mexican shandy** by using 1 part limeade and 1 part beer with the tequila and apricot nectar.

El Arándano Ágrio

Arándano is Spanish for cranberry, and that is the feature of this neat little cocktail. Not only does la arándano make a stunning display as an elegant cocktail glass filled with a brilliant red elixir, but it is stunning on the inside as well. Beauty in, beauty out.

Unlike the passion cocktail where the cranberry is merely an accent, here it is the golden star of the show, with the reposado tequila and ginger liqueur playing supporting roles. The tequila sweetens the deal, and the ginger is the spicy sidekick. The agave nectar and lime are extras used to fill the tasty scene.

When all of these characters are allowed to play their respective parts, the cocktail show is one to rival a masterpiece — suspenseful, sweet, tangy, and, overall, a beautiful dance in the mouth. As an extra treat, the candied ginger can be either dropped into the drink or laid out on the rim for the drinker to enjoy on its own.

- *1 ½ fl. oz. reposado tequila*
- *½ fl. oz. ginger liqueur*
- *2 fl. oz. cranberry juice*
- *¼ fl. oz. fresh lime juice*
- *Splash agave nectar*

Pour the ingredients into a cocktail shaker filled with ice. Shake and strain into a well-chilled cocktail glass.
Garnish: candied ginger

Tips

- You can make your own candied (or crystallized) ginger quite easily. Many recipes and tutorials are available; all you need is ginger, sugar, and water.

- If you have a long, thin piece of ginger, fold it over itself on a skewer to make a sort of ginger ribbon, adding a cherry in one of the folds.

Variations:

1. Offer guests the option of fruit in this cocktail. Pineapple and mango juices are two great alternatives to cranberry.

2. Make **la pera** by using pear nectar in place of the cranberry, and interlace thin pear slices in the garnish folds.

3. Add even more spice by topping the drink with a splash of ginger beer or the tamer ginger ale.

Kiwi-Strawberry Rustico

Rustic and simplistic? Yes. A drink to pass up? No. The drink that inspired this one — the classic old-fashioned — has proven over and over that straightforward drinks are sometimes the best when they are open to interpretation.

The whiskey-based old-fashioned is as contentious in construction as the martini and the margarita. Every ingredient has been brought into question, and rather silly, though heated, arguments have grown over this seemingly slick cocktail.

In the spirit of its patriarch, I have created the base rustico as a suggestion and invite your personal touches. The kiwi, strawberry, and añejo tequila with aromatic bitters is the way I enjoy it. The fruits complement the older tequila, yet allow it to radiate in its own distinct way. They are also sweet enough that a mere dash of nectar is needed.

I am not a stickler for my own recipes for either the old-fashioned or rustico. At times I will top the kiwi-strawberry rustico with a splash of seltzer, or in a friskier mood I may choose ginger ale. Depending on the season, I may switch out fruits to take advantage of rare finds, and at times I may use an infused simple syrup like the one made with potable rose water, which I often keep in stock.

- 2 slices kiwi, halved
- 1 strawberry, sliced
- 2 dashes aromatic bitters
- Dash amber agave nectar
- 2 fl. oz. añejo tequila

In the bottom of an old-fashioned glass, muddle the kiwi, strawberry, bitters, and nectar. Fill the glass with ice cubes and top with tequila. Stir, then squeeze a lemon twist over the top before laying it in the drink as a garnish.
Garnish: lemon twist

Variations:

1. Make a **star fruit–berry rustico** by substituting the fruits accordingly.

2. In deep winter you will find pomelo and tangerine. Muddle either with a cherry or lemon peel for a **citrus rustico**.

3. Labor-intensive, but worth it, try a **rhubarb rustico**. Make a rhubarb simple syrup with clean, 1-inch pieces of rhubarb. Strain the syrup and save the rhubarb, allowing both to cool completely. Muddle the syrup, 2–3 pieces of the rhubarb, and a sliced strawberry, and build the drink as noted.

Frambuesa Divina

Raspberry season is the time to seize the opportunity to use the delightful little fruits in a fresh raspberry cocktail like this frambuesa divina. The drink name translates into English as "raspberry divine," though I prefer the air of elegance in the Spanish name.

Raspberries are one of the easiest fruits to puree and are, well, divine in cocktails. Place about a cup of fresh, clean berries into a blender and puree until smooth. There will be miniscule pieces of the berries left in the puree, giving the drink a nice texture.

I chose to double up on the spirits here because raspberry is a nice complement to both reposado tequila and a good Cognac. The fruit acts as the missing link in the chain between the two liquors. Conversely, the earthy agave of the rested tequila and the sweet grape and oak of the brandy are the perfect background for the sweet fruit. It's the give-and-take relationship necessary in any cocktail.

- *1 fl. oz. reposado tequila*
- *1 fl. oz. Cognac*
- *¾ fl. oz. raspberry puree*
- *½ fl. oz. orange curaçao*
- *Juice from ½ lime*
- *3 dashes orange bitters*

Combine the ingredients in a cocktail shaker filled with ice. Shake vigorously and strain into a frozen cocktail glass.
Garnish: skewer of raspberries

Tips

- If they are available, add golden raspberries to the puree and alternate red and golden berries on the garnish skewer.

- Curaçao, or another light orange liqueur, is used here because of the brandy. A liqueur with the same base would be overkill on that flavor profile.

Variations:

1. Enhance the flavor by using the bitter herbal liqueur Jägermeister in place of the curaçao.

2. Create a **melocotón divina** by using a peach puree in place of the raspberries. Try white peaches or a puree of different peach varietals.

3. For a different accent, switch to grapefruit or chocolate bitters in any of these drinks.

Verde Fizz

The verde fizz was inspired by my green lemonade recipe, a nonalcoholic drink of kiwi, simple syrup, and both lemonade and limeade. You can serve it to the kids and any nondrinkers at your summer party, while making the verde fizz for the imbibers. It is an easy way to share the delights of kiwi with a diverse crowd.

In the verde fizz, I found that reposado tequila does the job. Its subtle sweetness and oak center the drink, bringing balance to the whole.

Kiwis are one of my favorite fruits, and muddling them is my prefered way to add their fresh taste to cocktails. Peel them first, then quarter the slices so they do not block the strainer.

Skip the egg if you like, or use an artificial egg-white substitute. In experiments with many substitutes, however, I have found them less desirable than an egg-free drink. Pasteurized eggs are, on most occasions, safe to drink raw. We add egg whites to cocktails because of the silky texture they create and the reaction this gives when soda is added. They are a "required" ingredient in traditional fizzes and many other old-time cocktails.

- 4 slices kiwi, quartered
- ½ fl. oz. simple syrup
- 1½ fl. oz. reposado tequila
- 1 egg white
- 4 fl. oz. limeade
- Club soda

Muddle the kiwi and simple syrup in the bottom of a cocktail shaker. Add ice, tequila, egg white, and limeade. Shake vigorously, strain into an ice-filled highball glass, and top with club soda.
Garnish: kiwi slice

Tips
- Shake any egg cocktail for at least 30 seconds to ensure the egg is properly integrated with the other ingredients.

- Limeade can be made fresh in the same manner as lemonade. Use twice as many limes because they are smaller than lemons.

Variations:
1. A **kumquat fizz** is made in the same manner, using kumquat in place of the kiwi.

2. For a **pear fizz**, skip the kiwi, muddle pear and ginger slices with syrup, and add ½ fl. oz. vanilla liqueur.

3. For a **mandarin fizz**, muddle mandarin orange slices with syrup, switch to fresh lemonade, and add ½ fl. oz. amaretto liqueur.

Jalisco Tea

One evening during a tour of distilleries in Jalisco, I left the bustling dinner party at the hacienda and wandered out into the agave field surrounding the distillery. I sipped the bartender's Jalisco tea as I watched the sun set over the blue-tinted hills covered in young agave. It was lovely and, when I returned home, I tried to capture that experience in a glass.

Though I do have the bartender's recipe from that evening, I made a few changes in my Jalisco tea. There is nothing too spectacular or exotic about it. It is an iced-tea drink, and as many before and since have proven, these are best left to a simple design. There is always room for experimentation, however, because of the variety of teas and herbal tisanes available, so with this base an endless number of flavors are possible.

My Jalisco tea begins with a reposado tequila and chilled green tea. The accent from the cherry liqueur is one that I often switch out, depending on the mood of the day. When tastes are running drier, the clear maraschino liqueur (specifically Luxardo) is ideal. Having nothing to do with the faux red cherries, this liqueur is made from the Marasca cherry and tends to have a bitter, almost almond-like flavor. For times when a sweeter Jalisco tea is called for, go with the darker Cherry Heering. This brand started back in 1818, was used in many classic cocktails, and has a modern following. It is distilled from black cherries and is just sweet enough to not overpower the drink. Cherry liqueurs beyond those two tend to be overtly sweet or bitter, and remind me too much of the cough syrups of childhood.

- 2 fl. oz. reposado tequila
- 1 fl. oz. cherry liqueur
- ¼ fl. oz. agave nectar
- Juice of ½ lime
- Fresh-brewed green tea, chilled

To a highball glass filled with ice, add each of the ingredients. Stir well, garnish, and serve with a straw.
Garnish: sprig of fresh herb and/or a lemon twist

Tips
- Garnish this tea with a fresh sprig from one of your herb plants. Rosemary, any variety of mint, lemon balm or verbena, and lavender are all good options that will gently infuse into the tea.
- A lemon or lime wedge or wheel can be served alongside the tea, giving the drinker the option to add more citrus if desired.
- Brew your tea with hot (not boiling) water and chill it thoroughly for the most intense flavor.

Variations:

1. As fruits come and go with the seasons, try muddling them with the nectar before building the rest of the drink. Berries are best for this.

2. For a lighter, very uplifting version, try substituting Yellow Chartreuse for the cherry liqueur and using a tea with a concentration of lemon.

3. At the other end of the spectrum, use Benedictine liqueur instead of the cherry liqueur and brew Earl Grey tea to make an intriguing, darker Jalisco tea.

Papaya Chispa

Tequila has a sophisticated side that sometimes goes unrecognized. The papaya chispa is a fine example of the spirit's potential in chic cocktails. Papaya season coincides with the summer months when tastes turn toward the tropics, so this version is ideal for warm-weather celebrations.

I chose papaya for the chispa (the word means *sparkle*) because many people, myself included, consider it a more exotic fruit. Like Champagne, I think of papaya when it comes to a special occasion for which you bring out the "good stuff." It is also a perfect fruit to make into a ball that ends up floating amongst all of the bubbles for a fun effect.

The spectacular part of the papaya chispa is in the presentation. It is essential to finish preparing the drink at the last moment, so guests can enjoy the reaction that happens inside the glass. When the sugar hits just-poured Champagne, it slowly dissolves, and a barrage of bubbles floats to the top. It is a captivating visual that doesn't last long, but it has been the appeal of the Champagne cocktail and has pleased drinkers for over 200 years. In keeping with the tradition of my chispa's predecessor, it is important to saturate the sugar with bitters. As the sugar mixes into the drink, it takes the bitters along for the ride and integrates the ingredients perfectly.

- *1 papaya ball*
- *1 ½ fl. oz. pineapple-infused blanco tequila or non-infused reposado tequila*
- *1 sugar cube*
- *2 dashes orange bitters*
- *Champagne or other sparkling wine*

Place the papaya ball, which you made with a melon baller from the flesh of a seeded papaya, into the bottom of a Champagne flute. Add tequila. Soak a sugar cube with bitters. When ready to serve, fill the glass with Champagne and drop the sugar cube inside.

Garnish: lemon spiral and star fruit

Tip

- An easy way to saturate a sugar cube with bitters is to place the cube on top of an open bottle of bitters. Turn the bottle upside down and give it a couple of shakes to release a few drops directly onto the cube.

Variations:

1. Make a **tequila mimosa** by mixing 1½ fl. oz. tequila and 2 fl. oz. fresh-squeezed orange juice and topping the flute with Champagne.

2. Try an **amor frizzante**. Build 1½ fl. oz. tequila and 1 fl. oz. each orange liqueur and peach nectar in a flute, topping it with Prosecco.

3. An entirely different twist is a **café chispa**. Pour 1½ fl. oz. coffee-infused blanco tequila, 1 fl. oz. amaretto, and ½ fl. oz. simple syrup in a glass, topping it off with any sparkling wine.

Melon Cocoa Drizzle

Green cocktails are fascinating and appealing, and have a sense of mystery about them. Rather unique in the cocktail world, their color is derived from only a few sources, typically melon liqueur or apple schnapps.

Midori is the best-known melon liqueur and a staple for a well-stocked bar. Imitations are available, but none stands up to its premium taste, which is surprisingly refreshing and not overly sweet. This profile has landed Midori in cocktails containing a whole host of flavors and has allowed it to be featured many times as the lone spirit in drinks. It is also stunning to look at.

In the melon cocoa drizzle, I have played to the strengths of the melon, pairing it with blanco tequila as is done in a Midori margarita. To make the flavor more interesting, I added a little elderflower liqueur to enhance the floral side of the tequila. In the spirit of a visually stimulating drink, I have also added a chocolate drizzle in the glass.

- *Chocolate syrup*
- *1 ½ fl. oz. blanco tequila*
- *1 ½ fl. oz. Midori melon liqueur*
- *½ fl. oz. St-Germain elderflower liqueur*
- *Juice of ½ lemon*
- *¼ fl. oz. agave nectar*

Prepare a cocktail glass by drizzling the chocolate syrup around the inside in a spiral, adding as little or as much as you like. Place the glass in the freezer. Combine the remaining ingredients in a cocktail shaker filled with ice and shake well. Strain into the prepared glass.

Garnish: chocolate syrup drizzle and green sugar for rimming

Tips

- For more control, transfer the chocolate syrup from its original bottle into a thin-tipped squeeze bottle. Squeeze it gently to create a light, even stream of chocolate, and avoid any large puddles of chocolate.

- If you opt for the sugar rim (see Embellishments on page 99), do it before adding the chocolate syrup.

Variations:

1. Add to the herbaceous flavor by using a tequila infused with lemongrass.

2. An **apricot cocoa drizzle** is delicious. Simply use apricot liqueur in place of the melon. The color will be a brilliant orange.

3. Similarly, a **mango cocoa drizzle** is made with mango liqueur or nectar. Many premium options are available, and most give the drink a pale orange-yellow color similar to orange juice.

Mint Madre

If you have ever enjoyed the tempting aroma of the pineapple mint plant, then you'll love the mint madre. For those unfamiliar with the herb, you will find it to be one of the best fruit-herb combinations available. I thoroughly enjoy making the mint madre because it is so fragrant and instantly brightens the mood of any room.

The mint madre is to blanco tequila what the rustico is to añejo. Notice the use of lighter flavors with the lighter tequila. They brighten up the spirit, enhancing its natural profile, and allowing the agave to really sparkle. This is one of the most refreshing drinks you will taste and can be made taller and effervescent with a little club soda.

Peppermint and spearmint are the most common varieties of mint, but it is fun to use other mints in the mint madre. Apple mint, ginger mint, and orange mint are good choices that bring a rather interesting and unique depth to the drink. Other hybrids like chocolate mint, lavender mint, sweet lemon mint, and, of course, pineapple mint work as well. Creative gardeners are continually cultivating new mint varieties, and almost any of them is a delight here because the drink has such a clean base.

- *Leaves from a sprig of mint, torn*
- *4–5 pineapple cubes*
- *2 dashes orange bitters*
- *Dash clear agave nectar*
- *2 fl. oz. blanco tequila*

In the bottom of an old-fashioned glass, muddle the mint, pineapple, bitters, and nectar. Fill the glass with ice cubes, top with tequila, and stir.
Garnish: maraschino cherry–pineapple-mint flag

Tips

- To make the cherry-pineapple-mint "flag" seen in the photograph, skewer together a pineapple wedge, mint leaves, and a cherry.

- Other citrus bitters like grapefruit and lemon are fantastic options.

Variations:

1. Add a little spice by placing a serrano chile slice into the muddle.

2. Make a **cherry-mint madre** by using cherry-infused tequila. Hint: Score the cherry's flesh for maximum flavor.

3. Use papaya to its fullest potential by infusing the spicy seeds into simple syrup. Replace the nectar with ½ fl. oz. of the infused syrup. Then muddle diced papaya in place of the pineapple.

Dulce de Arandas

■■ ■ ■■■ ■■ ■■

Luxury in a glass: this is the best way to describe the dulce de Arandas. *Dulce* means "sweet," and Arandas is the municipality in Jalisco, Mexico, with a booming tequila industry where many of my favorite tequilas are produced. I did design the dulce de Arandas to satiate the sweet tooth of the drinker, though it is not one of those excessively sweet cocktails. Instead, its crafted layering of ingredients combines into a delectable mix.

The tequila I recommend here is a blanco, because I have added whiskey, which brings in the taste of barrel aging, so aged tequila is too much of that profile. There are many strawberry liqueurs, but I recommend avoiding the cream and crème options, as they are too sweet and thick. Instead, choose a strawberry such as Bols or Fragoli, which use natural ingredients and often have evidence of the berries left in the bottle, to create an *au naturel* texture in the cocktail.

Chocolate bitters are a finishing touch, which I deem essential. They are not sweet and their effect is miniscule, though they bind all of the other ingredients together and act as a mediator between the tequila and whiskey.

- *1 ½ fl. oz. blanco tequila*
- *1 ½ fl. oz. bourbon whiskey*
- *½ fl. oz. strawberry liqueur*
- *Splash agave nectar*
- *Splash fresh lime juice*
- *2–3 dashes chocolate bitters*

Pour the ingredients into a cocktail shaker filled with ice. Shake well and strain into a chilled cocktail glass.
Garnish: chocolate-covered strawberry (see Tips below)

Tips

- An alternative to strawberry liqueur is a fresh strawberry puree.

- Either orange or grapefruit bitters will work as well.

- Make chocolate-covered strawberries by melting chocolate chips in a microwave for about 1½ minutes. Place strawberries on a skewer, dip into the chocolate, and twirl slowly. Allow them to cool, suspending them by the skewer if possible.

- Cut a small slit into the strawberry so it rests on the rim of the glass.

Variation:

- Convert this recipe into a **black raspberry delight** by using Chambord instead of strawberry.

Envy

The envy was my first neat tequila cocktail besides the margarita, and it remains a favorite. Just like the green-colored cocktails, blue drinks are too much fun to pass by. When someone sets an elegant blue cocktail like this in front of you, it has the ability to put a smile on your face immediately.

It is a beautiful reminder of tropical waters and moments in the sun, and the taste reflects that feeling. The three simple ingredients combine to transport you to the beach straightaway, and I often use an envy to beat the midwinter blues, as a reminder that there is sun and sand out there somewhere.

Blue liqueurs are rare. Two of the most common are blue curaçao and Hpnotiq. The former is called for in the common envy recipe because it is a deeper blue, and its orange flavor is a natural companion for pineapple and tequila. I have made the envy with Hpnotiq, and it makes an equally fantastic drink, though it has an entirely different flavor. Hpnotiq has a vodka and Cognac base, flavored with a "secret" blend of tropical juices.

- *1½ fl. oz. blanco tequila*
- *¾ fl. oz. blue curaçao*
- *¾ fl. oz. pineapple juice*
- *Dash orange bitters*

Pour the ingredients in a cocktail shaker filled with ice. Shake well and strain into a frozen cocktail glass filled with cracked ice.
Garnish: pineapple flag or single cherry

Tips

- When shaken, pineapple juice adds a lovely foam to the drink.

- Blue curaçao is also available as a nonalcoholic mixer. This is a great option for making blue virgin drinks for the kids, but is too sweet and unnecessary for cocktails.

- This is one of the few drinks served in a cocktail glass that calls for ice (be sure to use cracked ice). Feel free to serve it neat also.

Variations:

1. Make the envy into a drier cocktail by adding ½ fl. oz. dry vermouth to the recipe and foregoing the ice.

2. Add a little more fruit flavor with a splash of maraschino liqueur.

3. Get a similar color with a different flavor by using orange juice instead of pineapple.

Romero Collins

There is a formula for drinks that fall into the classic "collins" family: base spirit, lemon, sugar, soda. This simple recipe has been adapted many times over the years. Think of the tom collins (gin), john collins (whiskey), juan collins (tequila), and vodka collins. While they are all essentially the same drink, the liquor base brings a whole new twist to each.

I've taken the "collins theory" a step further in the romero collins. Here we show off the beauty of the juan collins and enhance it with rosemary, which is a personal favorite when it comes to herbs. The marriage of tequila and rosemary is a fascinating one — after one taste, it seems that the two are a match made in heaven.

It takes less than a week to obtain a well-balanced rosemary-infused tequila. Use 2–3 full sprigs of rosemary for a 750ml bottle of blanco tequila.

- 2 fl. oz. rosemary-infused tequila
- 1 fl. oz. fresh-squeezed lemon juice
- 4 fl. oz. agave nectar
- Club soda

Pour the tequila, lemon juice, and agave nectar into a cocktail shaker filled with ice. Shake well and strain into an ice-filled collins glass.
Garnish: rosemary sprig and lemon peel

Tips

- Since you are already infusing the tequila, why not try out some flavored sweeteners? Substitute flavored simple syrup for the agave nectar for another splash of flavor. Flavors to consider include lavender, tangerine, ginger, and vanilla bean. (See page 31 for more ideas.)

- Cut your lemon peel for the garnish first, then use the rest of the lemon to squeeze for the juice in the drink.

Variations:

1. Revert to a non-infused blanco (or better yet, reposado) tequila to make the more common **juan collins**.

2. For a slightly sweeter version, try a **granada collins**. Add ½ fl. oz. of either pomegranate liqueur or juice to the original recipe.

3. Create a **jengibre collins** by substituting ginger ale for the club soda. For an even spicier ginger flavor, use a Jamaican ginger beer.

Tequila Café

Though it is rare, tequila can make a great warm drink. We just have to be picky about how it is used. The tequila café is inspired by Irish coffee and is made in the same manner — complete with a whipped cream and chocolate topping.

In the tequila café, a blanco or reposado will do just fine. The amaretto plays the role of the middle guy, balancing the tequila and coffee. The almond flavor is a common addition to coffee drinks, and without it here you simply have tequila-spiked coffee in which something is obviously missing. That extra ingredient can be any number of liqueurs, some of which appear in the variations below. The key to choosing one is its ability to complement both ingredients and not become the forward flavor.

Coffee . . . The brew from your kitchen's drip coffeemaker will do, but in my world, that coffee is relegated to the occasional morning cup. Most of the time — and always when making coffee cocktails — I use my trusted French press and a dark roast, freshly ground bean. The resulting coffee is rich, creamy, thick, and full of flavor — just how I like it — and ideal for mixing with any spirit.

- 2 fl. oz. tequila
- 1 fl. oz. amaretto liqueur
- Fresh-brewed cinnamon coffee

Pour the tequila and amaretto into a warmed Irish coffee glass or mug and fill with freshly brewed coffee. Top with a mound of whipped cream and drizzle of chocolate syrup.

Garnish: whipped cream and chocolate syrup

Tips

- Make cinnamon coffee by adding crushed cinnamon sticks to the coffee grounds while brewing.
- The longer you allow coffee to brew in a French press before depressing the plunger, the stronger and more caffeinated it is.
- Warm your glass or mug by simply filling it with hot water for a few minutes.

Variations:

1. In place of the amaretto, use ½ fl. oz. each vanilla and coffee liqueurs.

2. Make a **café de nuez** by using Frangelico or another nutty liqueur instead of amaretto.

3. Turn this into an iced coffee by chilling the coffee, building the drink over ice, and adding milk as desired.

A sample variety of tequila bottles with a shot of añejo tequila in a caballito glass

Shots & Shooters

We could not talk about tequila without throwing a few tequila shots into the mix, now could we? You are in the bar with a group of friends and order "a round of tequila shots." What do you get? Typically, whatever the establishment has stocked in their well. This could be any number of tequilas and is usually the cheapest in the house. Sometimes it is a blanco, sometimes a gold tequila. The gold tequila option is likely the tequila that tainted your tequila-drinking dreams years ago.

My advice is to ask the bartender what is available for premium blancos or reposados, and fork over the few extra bucks to seriously improve your experience.

Barspeak: *"Would you like training wheels with that?"*

Interpretation: *"Do you want lemon/lime and salt?"*

"Training wheels" (or tequila cruda) refers to the salt and citrus taken on either side of the tequila shot. They are used to make the shot easier to take and to enhance its flavors, though it began over a century ago in Mexico as a way to take tequila as medicine.

The process is as follows:

- Lick or moisten the back of your hand (a lemon or lime wedge is good) between the index finger and thumb, and pour salt on it.
- Lick the salt off your hand.
- Take the shot of tequila.
- Immediately bite into and suck the juice from the lemon or lime wedge.

Think: lick-sip-suck.

The salt lessens the burn of the tequila and alerts your taste buds to the oncoming strong flavor. The fruit is sour and balances and enhances the flavor of the tequila. Not all tequilas or tequila drinkers require these flavor buffers, but the process is fun in a group.

My philosophy on shots and shooters is simple: they should taste good. The days of appalling shooters — in taste, appearance, and name — are over, and though shots may not be as common as they once were, I see no reason that they should not be as tasty as a cocktail. It is just as important, in fact, because a shooter is a single moment in time that will leave you with either a pleasant, satisfied feeling or force you to show your friends the worst face you have, only to find a picture of it online a week later. There are no "maybe

Reposado tequila in a caballito glass

the drink will get better toward the bottom of the glass" thoughts allowed with shooters; they're done and over with in an instant and have the ability to make or break the rest of your evening.

When it comes to shooters, I have a little test for tastiness. If it can be poured over ice and the drinker can spend the next 20 minutes enjoying it, it is a keeper. If, however, the drinker cannot get past the first sip, it is time to return to the mixology drawing board.

The glassware choice is also important with tequila shots. Yes, a short shot glass will do, but using the tall, slender caballitos (like those in the photograph opposite) is not only more traditional to tequila's Mexican roots, but is a little classier.

The next question is whether to use a lemon or a lime. Many Americans prefer lemon and go with that. However, as I said previously, lime is a far better complement to tequila. If you are serving a round with training wheels, give each taker the option by offering both. Also, I like the idea of placing small piles of salt — one for each person — on a plate. They can lick the tip of their index finger, dip it into their own salt pile, lick, and proceed.

Embellishments

Without the training wheels, you may consider enhancing tequila shots by rimming each glass with:

- A mix of equal parts sugar and ground cinnamon.

- Cracked pepper added to rimming salt in a ratio of about 1 part pepper to 2 parts salt.

- Colored sugars (such as the yellow sugar in the photograph opposite) — found in the supermarket's baking section — or a mix of two or more colors to fit the occasion.

Tequila shots in caballitos: (from left to right) blanco tequila with yellow sugar rim, reposado tequila with salt rim, añejo tequila with sugar and cinnamon rim

Diablo's Licor

Sweet, spicy, and far too tempting, this is diablo's licor. A snappy little shooter with an explosion of flavor, it is a joy to share with friends.

In keeping with the multifaceted tradition of tequila shooters, I have designed diablo's licor as not just a drink, but a process. We have, on one hand, a shot glass filled with a luscious liquid that tantalizes the palate with the exotic flair of passion fruit. On the other hand, we have a fiery morsel that rocks your world. Sometimes opposites do attract, and this shooter is proof.

Let us begin at the end. In the shot glass is a combination of tequila, lime, and passion fruit. It is a delicate mix that I would serve in a cocktail glass any day of the week. The tequila I use is a premium blanco, though if you feel the need, go with a reposado. Fresh lime juice is essential, and if you have a juicer, do not hesitate to make fresh passion fruit juice as well. Though commercial passion fruit juices are available, they can be a challenge to locate (but the reward of this hunt is well worth it).

The true devil of diablo's licor is the pepper. I will warn you that this shooter is not for the faint of heart; it is for the lover of spice and contrast. Choose a pepper that is not too spicy — this is not a challenge, but an experience — so a jalapeño, serrano, or other milder chile pepper will do just fine. You are going to begin by eating a whole slice to jump-start your taste buds, and then following it with the enticing contents of the shooter, which will extinguish whatever fire is burning in your mouth. Enjoy the flavors.

- 1 fl. oz. blanco tequila
- 1 fl. oz. passion fruit juice
- ½ fl. oz. fresh lime juice

Cut a slice of pepper, remove the seeds and pulp, and then skewer each slice on a cocktail pick. Pour the liquids into a cocktail shaker filled with ice, shake well, and strain into a shot glass. Lay the skewered pepper on top of the glass. Garnish: hot pepper slice

Tips

- Prepare the peppers, one for each person, beforehand and wash your hands thoroughly. The peppers are skewered so that the drinkers can take their bite without touching the pepper, and this avoids the potential of burning their skin or eyes.

- Do avoid habanero or any of the really hot peppers. This is meant to be a "mild" spice, not a five-alarm fire in your mouth.

Variations:

1. Instead of using lime juice, use ½ fl. oz. of simple syrup infused with Meyer lemon.

2. Add more fruit flavors by infusing the tequila with berries or apricot.

3. Switch out the juices: instead of passion fruit, use orange or pineapple juice, or a combination of the two.

El Tigre

El tigre is a simple shooter that is packed with flavor. Though they originate from opposite parts of the world, lychee (pronounced *lee-chee*) and tequila are a natural pairing, because the delicate fruit sweetens the more vegetal agave flavor. The cranberry accents both flavors and gives the shooter a beautiful crimson color.

What is a lychee, you ask? It is a sweet little fruit, native to most of tropical Asia. Though the trees are somewhat rare, the fruit can often be found canned in Asian markets. You may also come across the fresh fruit, which has a red husk similar in shape and color to a strawberry (they are also called "alligator strawberries"). Inside is the sweet, white flesh that is the real fruit.

It was not long ago that lychee was introduced to a broader market of cocktail drinkers via a variety of liqueurs and mixers. It was the trendy new "superfruit" for a little while. Most of the liqueurs were clear colored, though a few were a beautiful, deep pink. Many of the brands went by the wayside shortly after, though there are still a few available. Soho is probably the most widely distributed, but if you find another lychee liqueur, seize the moment and buy it.

This lychee cocktail trend left us with some fabulous drinks that many people continue to enjoy. I like to take advantage of those flavor fads to explore new tastes, and the lychee is a perfect example. That is why, years later, I continue to hold el tigre as a personal favorite.

- *1 ½ fl. oz. blanco tequila*
- *½ fl. oz. lychee liqueur*
- *½ fl. oz. cranberry juice*

Combine the ingredients in a cocktail shaker filled with ice and shake well. Strain into a tall shot glass.
Garnish: small lime wedge

Tip
- Cut a lime wheel and slice it as you would a pizza for tiny wedges, which are the perfect size for this shooter.

Variations:

1. Substitute TY KU or Hpnotiq liqueur for the lychee. TY KU is another Asian-inspired spirit with a sake base, an almost neon green color, and a delicious flavor made from a blend of 20 fruits and botanicals. Hpnotiq is just as captivating in color, with its brilliant blue, and is made from a proprietary blend of fruits with vodka and Cognac. To show off the color of either of those liqueurs, use a white cranberry juice instead of red.

2. Substitute Jägermeister for the lychee liqueur. Though Jägermeister often gets a bad rap because of its association with harsh-tasting shooters, it is a pleasant complement when used correctly. Cranberry is one of those flavors that does a wonderful job of taming the potent herbs.

3. Play with a variety of fruit juices. You'll find that the lychee is one of those fruits that pairs nicely with almost any other fruit, and that versatility is perfect for experimentation with this shooter. Suggestions for fruit substitutions include raspberry, white grape, grapefruit, tangerine, and apricot.

Sangrita

Sangrita is not necessarily a shooter, but a chaser to a shot of tequila. The name means "little blood," and it has been the preferred palate cleanser between sips in Mexico since the 1920s. It is only recently that this mild mix found its way outside of the Jalisco area. The traditional method is to alternate sips (not shots) from the two glasses, allowing the sangrita to cool the pepper of the tequila and to clean the palate.

There are two recipes for sangrita. The more traditional of the two comes straight out of Guadalajara. It is said to have derived from the leftover juices used for pico de gallo, which is as popular there as sangrita. (Both recipes that follow should fill four caballitos.)

Adaptation of the traditional recipe:
- *4 fl. oz. fresh orange juice*
- *3 fl. oz. fresh lime juice*
- *2 fl. oz. grenadine or pomegranate juice*
- *6 dashes hot sauce or 1 tsp. chile pepper*

The accounts of how the second version came about are rather amusing. Supposedly, visitors taking the "recipe" home tried to account for the red color that came from the chile. Mistakenly, tomato juice was used.

Adaptation of the tomato recipe:
- *4 fl. oz. tomato juice*
- *3 fl. oz. fresh orange juice*
- *2 fl. oz. fresh lime juice*
- *1 tsp. chile pepper*

Of course, it does not end there. Many more adaptations have been made, and some of those are on the opposite page. The important ingredients are orange, lime, and some sort of spice, though even these are not always included.

To prepare any sangrita, place the ingredients in a cocktail shaker and shake *without* ice. Chill the mix in the refrigerator. Serve the sangrita in a caballito or other tall shot glass, alongside a matching glass filled with straight tequila.

Variations:

1. Mix 6 fl. oz. tomato juice, 2 fl. oz. each orange and lime juices, 1 teaspoon horseradish, and 1 jalapeño slice.

2. In a food processor, puree 6 fl. oz. tomato juice, 2 slices cucumber, 3 slices jalapeño, 2 slices ginger, and 1 fl. oz. each orange and lime juices.

3. Shake together 5 fl. oz. clamato, 1 fl. oz. lime juice, and 4 dashes each hot and Worcestershire sauces.

Firecracker

A sip of the firecracker shooter is like throwing a party in your mouth. It combines three ingredients that have a powerful personality of their own. When they mix, it is nothing short of an explosion of flavor.

The tequila should be a premium blanco of your choice. We are aiming for that raw taste of agave, with a little spice in the background. Goldschläger is my first choice any time cinnamon liqueur is called for. There are two reasons for this: in today's market, it is the smoothest cinnamon spirit available and is delicate enough in its flavor to play well with other ingredients, and there is the bonus of the gold flakes that float inside. In this instance the gold adds the sparkle necessary for the firecracker theme. The crème de menthe is included to add a little refreshment, and its intense cooling effect is a lovely contrast to the two other ingredients. Go with clear (or white) crème de menthe in order to maintain the clear liquid that makes this shooter look best.

- *1 fl. oz. blanco tequila*
- *1 fl. oz. Goldschläger*
- *½ fl. oz. white or clear crème de menthe*

Pour the ingredients directly into a shot glass. Give the drink a quick stir, using a straw.

Tips

- Notice that I do not shake this shooter before pouring. This is to retain as much of the gold as possible. If we were to shake, we could lose flakes in the shaker, amongst the ice, and during the strain.

- Use a jigger to measure the ingredients for an accurate pour. If some flakes are left behind in the jigger, they may be picked up by the crème de menthe.

Variations:

1. My favorite rendition of this shooter uses amaretto in place of the crème de menthe.

2. Another substitute for the mint is a honey liqueur such as Bärenjäger.

3. Turn the firecracker into a snappy fruit shooter by using apple schnapps instead of crème de menthe.

CHAPTER 4:

Tequila Production

■■ ■■ ■■ ■■ ■ ■

The creation of any mass-produced beverage is fascinating, and distilled spirits are no exception. Maybe it is a personal bias, but I think the distillation process is by far the most interesting and, of the liquors produced throughout the world, tequila is possibly the most intriguing. For *tequilleros* to transform an oversized, underground succulent into a liquid that is wholly unique as both a category and within each individual bottling is simply amazing. Many of the methods employed remain traditional. Let us look at how this Mexican field-to-glass process goes.

In the Fields

Tequila begins in the fields of Mexico at least eight years before a bottle is ready to hit the shelves. My first encounter with this unique agriculture began in flight on my first trip to the tequila region of Jalisco. The familiar color of the North American farming landscape slowly transforms from those shades of greens and browns to a subtle blue. First there is a patch of blue every few miles, and it appears to be an unnatural phenomenon — maybe due to some farmer's weird experiment — then the blue fields multiply until they take over the entire landscape below. It is at this point that you know you are in the land where the agave grows and tequila reigns supreme.

The breathtaking landscape of the Mexican state that produces the majority of tequila is a wonder to behold, but it is not until you are standing on the ground surrounded by head-high agave plants that true appreciation for tequila can be found. Tequila production is one of the most labor-intensive among distilled spirits, and it begins in these fields. According to the CRT (Tequila Regulatory Council), a December 2010 inventory of Weber blue agave estimated that 253 million plants were in various stages on nearly 95,000 hectares of plantation lands. That is a lot of agave! Each mature

Harvesting blue agave

A field of blue agave in Jalisco, Mexico

plant weighs between 50 and 150 pounds at harvest. Considering that it takes 10–15 pounds of that raw agave to produce one 750ml bottle of tequila, that is a lot of potential tequila in these fields. The immensity of the landscape is overwhelming as well as beautiful.

The agave fields are as diverse as the tequilas they produce. In the area around the town of Tequila in the Sierra Madre foothills, the soil is filled with volcanic rock and other unique minerals. The contrast is seen best when one travels to the highlands of Jalisco around the town of Arandas, where the iron-oxide soil is a brilliant red in shocking contrast to the blue plants. Ownership of the plantations varies as well. Many of the smaller, boutique distilleries will plant their own fields surrounding the production facilities, while many of the larger producers will contract out to individual farmers whose fields may be miles away.

Agave tequilana Weber azul, or Weber blue agave, is the primary source for tequila. By law, all tequilas must be made from at least 51% of this particular species of agave plant, with the best tequilas made of it entirely (labeled 100% blue agave). The agave has the appearance of a cactus, complete with spiny, barb-tipped leaves that will definitely leave a mark if one is not careful, which is why it is a common misconception that it is a cactus. The agave plant is actually a member of the Agavaceae family, a succulent that looks more like an aloe vera plant on steroids, and includes around 300 different species. They can grow over 6 feet tall, and their rosette pattern of leaves can have a diameter of about that size. At full maturity, agave are awe-inspiring plants.

As impressive as agave are aboveground, it is the unseen that is the treasure that will be transformed into tequila. After 7 to 12 years of growth, *jimadores*, or fieldworkers, determine if each plant is ready for harvest. When a plant is selected, the jimadore uses a round, razor-sharp tool called a coa to remove some of the base leaves before extracting the whole plant from the ground. The prize is the massive ball, called a *piña*, which emerges. More work is done to remove every leaf from the piña using the coa, leaving behind the clean heart of the agave, which looks like a gigantic, green and white pineapple.

The task of harvesting cannot be discounted as a simple or easy one. There is no modern machinery that can take the place of the (often generational) jimadore, and there is no shortcut that can be taken to get this dangerous job done. I had my chance to wield a coa and take a whack at the agave leaves. A few misplaced strikes of the heavy staff, and I knew it was a job best left to the professionals. The cuts must be carefully aimed at the base of each leaf while avoiding a gash into the piña flesh, and any other misplaced strikes can easily take off a finger, toe, or whatever is in its way. Relentless and strong, an experienced jimadore can clean a piña in a matter of minutes, averaging 50–60 in a day's work. The agave hearts are then loaded up and sent off to the distillery. Some travel in trucks, while others from the rockier slopes begin their journey from the fields on the backs of donkeys. The leaves are often left behind to decompose and fertilize the field for the next planting.

Cultivating agave plants is a year-round process. The cycle of planting, caring for, and harvesting must be continual

Agave piñas turn a sweet, syrupy brown after baking

because of the time it takes to grow each plant. In the fields you will see agave at various stages of growth, from the small transplants fresh from the greenhouse to the giants ready to harvest. Because of this continuing cycle and the growers' desire for consistency, tequila has no vintage where one year's production is better than another, as we often see in wine. Tequila producers are all about continuing the same taste from one year to the next. Agave take on the personality of their environment and climate, and tequila carries on that personality, so these rigorous methods are employed to retain that stability.

In the Distillery

A mix of traditional and modern methods continues in the distilleries. Each has its own interpretation of the process, with some distilleries following traditions that may be enhanced with modern technology and some that are fully mechanized, mass-producing their tequilas. Most use a mixture of the

Harvested agave piñas being loaded into an oven

two. In each step a distillery will define its process based on what is wanted for the tequila.

When the field-fresh heart of the agave reaches the distillery, the real tequila journey begins. The first step is to bake the hard agave so its rich juices can be extracted. Some distilleries will toss whole piñas in the ovens, while others begin by cutting them in half or quarters for easy handling. Traditional baking methods use stone-walled ovens. This requires a slower cooking time, averaging around three days to get a delicately roasted agave. The modern version employs enormous stainless-steel autoclaves in which the agave are in the pressure cooker for around 12 hours. Both styles of oven use steam to bake the hearts.

Before baking, the agave piñas are white and green, nearly as firm as a rock, and have a taste of bitter herb, which is hardly palatable. After baking, the agave are transformed into brown, fibrous lumps of syrupy candy and are absolutely delicious. While it can be likened to the sweetest of sweet potatoes, it retains that sweet, earthy agave flavor, which has no comparison.

Now that the agave's carbohydrates and starches have been transformed into fermentable sugars, it is time to extract the juice. Again, there is a split between traditional and modern techniques. Some very traditional distillers will include the fibers while fermenting, though most will ferment only the juice. The modern technique uses large machines that press every last drop of juice from the baked agave in a very quick process. A traditional method

The tahona wheel in an old tequila factory

uses a large stone wheel called a *tahona*. For this, the agave pulp is placed in a shallow pit with grooves that collect the juice. The tahona spins slowly around the pit, crushing and pressing out the juices while a worker follows behind, turning the agave and readying it for the next pass of the wheel. At one time, horses or donkeys pulled the tahonas around the circle; now they are mechanized and automatically continue a slow gait around and around until all of the juice has been collected. This is time consuming, but those who use the tahona swear by its superiority in producing the best agave juice.

Now the agave juice, which is full of sugar, is ready to be fermented. Depending on the distillery, fermentation may take place in either wood or stainless-steel tanks. When the tanks are full of the agave juice, yeasts are added and, if the tequila is meant to be a blend (or *mixto*), sugar syrups may be added as well. Every distillery throughout the world covets its yea st cultures, which are key to giving the liquor quite a bit of its character. Some yeast is commercially produced and some is wild. It is typical that once a yeast is found to achieve the desired output, it will be used for every batch of liquor in the future.

I find it amusing how some distilleries treat their fermenting juices. It is true that yeast is a living organism, and a handful of distillers will try to make it as comfortable as possible. This is why you may hear music piping through a room full of enormous fermentation tanks. I've heard classical orchestras, rock 'n' roll, and traditional mariachi tunes in use. One distiller told me that "happy yeast is productive yeast," so he's willing to accommodate and treat his cultures to the good vibes of the music that surrounds them. Though some very fine tequilas do not have this luxury, I'm willing to keep an open mind that there may be some psychological reaction in the tiny organisms.

At any rate, while fermenting, the yeast converts the agave sugars into mild alcohol similar to beer (or *pulque*). It does this over an average of 72 hours, during which the tank steadily becomes more active, simmering and bubbling and warming.

When fermentation is complete, it is time to hit the still and, again, distilleries will differ on method. The majority of tequila is distilled twice, though some does take a third trip through the still. Distilleries will use a traditional copper-pot still or the more modern stainless-steel continuous-column stills. Each style of still imparts different qualities to the alcohol, but the goal is the same. In distillation, the fermented "beer" is heated to a boil and vapors are released.

These vapors are captured and condensed into a clear liquid that is around 40% alcohol per volume. The heads and tails (top and bottom parts of the distillate) are removed because these tend to have the most impurities, and the heart (middle of the batch) is held for a second trip through the still. Heads and tails are once again removed, and we now have blanco tequila.

At this point, the tequila will take one of these paths:

- For a blanco tequila, the tequila may take a siesta for up to 60 days in stainless-steel tanks before bottling or go straight to the bottling line.

- For reposado and añejo tequilas, it's off to the barrel house for a rest of anywhere from three months to three years (or longer for extra-añejo), according to the style.

- Tequilas meant to be mixtos (such as gold tequilas) may be blended with other ingredients on-site or shipped en masse to a blending and bottling facility off-site, usually in the United States.

The Aging Process

The only requirements for aging tequila are the various times needed to obtain the type of tequila to be bottled, so the aging process varies by distillery (see pages 12-15). Barrel houses at tequila distilleries look no different than those for whiskey. In fact, used whiskey barrels often find their way to Mexico. This is especially true with bourbon barrels, which can be used only once and are then sold to other distilleries all over the world to age everything from other whiskies to tequilas and rums.

Why Is Tequila Not Aged as Long as Whiskies?

Because of climate, tequila (and most rums) does not require the 10–30 years of aging that many whiskies are given. The arid, hot weather of Mexico speeds the aging process when compared to the cool, moist climates of the north, where many whiskies are produced. If tequila was allowed to age for 10 years, it would lose all of its agave characteristics. These shorter aging times tend to make up for the longer growing times required of the agave plant, when put into perspective against other aged liquors.

UILA TEQUILA

CHAPTER 5:

Tequila Through Time

![decorative bar]

Tequila, like many alcoholic beverages with a thousand or more years under its belt, has roots in which divine intervention, inspiration, or purpose played a role in its creation. Its past is also comprised of years of folklore, poor historical records (by modern standards), and a hazy influence from the source itself. Yet these inconclusive tales throughout tequila's history add to its mystery and intrigue and, quite frankly, make for good bar talk. Though we cannot be entirely sure of the full story, there are some rather interesting tales of its origin.

Tequila's story dates back to pre-Hispanic times in the Chimalhuacán region. It is said that a few people from the Nahuatl tribe were collecting plants in a ravine during a tiring journey to the "promised land." Lightning struck an agave plant, and a fire spread across an entire field of the wild succulent. An unfamiliar fragrance filled the air and captivated the gatherers, who decided to investigate. Their delight at the sweet flavor they smelled led them to harvest the agave in an attempt to reproduce the cooked treat.

From this point the stories are unclear as to exactly how the Nahuatl came to ferment and distill an alcohol from their new discovery. Historians debate whether the beverage, which became known as "tepache mezcal," was the result of accidental fermentation from leftover baked agave or through knowledge acquired by tradition, trial and error, or maybe even divine intervention.

At any rate, the Nahuatl created a "wine" called pulque from the agave. It was not until the arrival of the Spanish conquistadors that distillation was thrown into the mix. Pulque was integrated into the Aztec culture, just as tequila is in today's Mexican culture.

When the Spaniards made it to the Chimalhuacán region during their 15th-century conquest of Mexico, they were intrigued by the Nahuatls' agave beverage. They decided to apply European distilling methods to make tepache

The Aztec Legend of Agave

While on a 'tequila tour' in Jalisco, a representative of the Tequila Regulatory Council told this story about the origin of the agave plant. It is one of a few tales that are told on the subject, and it is said that this story in particular demonstrates the soul-comforting properties found in tequila today.

The Aztecs believed that when the Earth bega, there was an evil goddess in the sky named Tzitzimitl who devoured light. She held the people in darkness, only giving them a little light when they performed human sacrifices in her name.

One of the Nahuatl men, Quetzalcoatl, grew tired of this, and one day he ascended to the sky to fight the goddess and stop the constant darkness. In his search he found, instead, Tzitzimitl's granddaughter, Mayahuel (the goddess of fertility), who had been kidnapped by her grandmother. He fell in love with Mayahuel, and instead of killing the evil goddess, he brought Mayahuel down to Earth to live with him.

When Tzitzimitl found out about Quetzalcoatl's bold act, she was angry and came to Earth to find the couple. The young lovers hid from the goddess but eventually ran out of places to hide in their human form, so they decided to transform into trees. The lovers stood next to each other like this for years, and when the wind blew their leaves, they caressed the other.

Infuriated and frustrated with her search, Tzitzimitl sent light-devouring stars out to search for the couple, and they were finally found. A fight began between the goddess and the couple, and the lovely Mayahuel was killed.

The outraged Quetzalcoatl returned to the sky and killed Tzitzimitl, and light came back to the Earth, but every night he would go to Mayahuel's grave and cry. Feeling sorry for the man, the other gods decided to give him something. On the site where Mayahuel was buried, a plant began to grow, and the gods gave it hallucinogenic properties that would comfort Quetzalcoatl's soul. The plant would come to be known as the maguey (or agave) plant, and remain a comfort for all who drank the beverages made from it.

mezcal, a stronger drink. With the help of *mestizos* — people of mixed European and Native American blood — they constructed pots that would work like primitive versions of the fermentation and distillation tanks used in Spain. The result of this new combination of European and North American tradition, knowledge, and culture became known as "mezcal wine." It was not until the late 1800s, however, that the alcohol would be called "tequila wine" and eventually "tequila," named after the town near the original Nahuatl village.

In 1530, the town of Santiago de Tequila was established. *Tequila* derives from the Nahuatl word for volcano — *tel* means hill and *quilla* for lava. The City of Guadalajara was established shortly after, in 1542, and this area became the epicenter of all mezcal and tequila production to come. In 1600, Don Pedro Sanchez de Tagle, the "father of tequila," established the first mezcal distillery in Hacienda Cuisillos and began cultivating agave. By 1608, the first mezcal wine taxes were enacted.

This was also the era when the Spanish were importing their own wines and, as the popularity of Mexican wines and mezcal wine grew, trade from the Old World declined. Thinking that this would not do, the first ban on manufacturing mezcal wine was enacted, but it was eventually lifted in order to collect taxes on the liquor that had gone underground. This scenario played out a few times over the next centuries for various reasons, with the Mexican people always coming out on top, though always with higher taxes to pay on their product. By this time, mezcal wine had become a tradition among the people, and they worked and fought hard to maintain their use and sale of it.

Mezcal spread throughout the area. It was commonly transported by horse and mule in wood barrels or leather pitchers. In the 1700s, Tequila was along the route to the newly opened port of San Blas, and business was booming. Shipments were also being sent to Mexico City, where mezcal had become quite popular.

In 1740, José Antonio de Cuervo applied for the first official license to produce mezcal wine at his tavern (*taberna*). It was customary that the mezcal factories, or *fábricas*, served a dual purpose, and the drink was also consumed on the grounds. In 1758, Cuervo received the grant from the King of Spain to grow agave, and in 1781 the taberna reported producing 800,000 liters of mezcal. Another ten-year ban on production began in 1785 to, once again, favor Spanish imports, but it was lifted by King Charles IV in 1795, and taxes were again levied against all alcohol. In that same year, Cuervo's son, José Maria Guadalupe Cuervo, received a license, and the tavern became the first legal distillery to produce mezcal.

From this point the industry grew, contracted, and grew more in various cycles. Aided by the 1810–21 Mexican War of Independence, during which soldiers were stocked with mezcal, the early days of the war were profitable. A downturn was seen when Acapulco took over the premier port status from San Blas. More distilleries were opening up, and agave plants were exported to Europe and its colonies throughout the world. When the Mexican-American War took place between 1846 and 1848, mezcal wagons followed the soldiers, and the drink was popular among soldiers on both sides. It was one good turn followed by a bad turn, one after another.

Revolutions within the industry were also taking place. Early in the 19th century, mezcals were introduced to wood-barrel aging. Around 1850, distilleries began moving their ovens aboveground, and this was when mezcal and tequila parted ways. Tequila began to form its own identity, and by the end of the century, most distilleries had switched over to tequila. In 1860, Jesús Flores was the first to bottle tequila in glass. These *damajuanas* were hand-blown, round bottles wrapped in agave fibers and holding 5 liters. Bottling developed further. By the end of the 1800s, small bottles called *pachoncitas* were created, which allowed the tequila drinker to carry the bottle in their pocket.

It was in 1873 that the Sauza-Cuervo rivalry for market dominance began. In that year, Don Cenobio Sauza purchased a few distilleries. Cuervo claimed to have shipped the first three barrels of tequila to the United States, though Sauza claims to have delivered eight barrels earlier that year. By 1880, Cuervo was selling 10,000 bottles each year to Guadalajara alone. In 1888, Sauza purchased La Preservancia (the main distillery today), and thirteen other distilleries soon followed.

More innovations came about in these decades. In 1862, the Tequila Herradura Distillery was established, and it introduced reposado tequila to the world. Sauza is reported to have realized that blue agave made the best tequila, and he is credited with the adaptation of using steam in the new aboveground ovens known as *hornos*. The steam not only remedied the problem of a lack of wood in the now deforested area, but also took the smoky taste out of tequila and allowed the smooth, true agave flavor to shine, further differentiating it from mezcal. The railroads increased the ability to export the products, and powered presses and mills sped up the process of extracting juices and replaced the traditional tahona wheel.

The name of the liquor under these refined techniques also came into question. In 1870, a group of the largest tequila producers approached the Mexican government to request that they be able to label their product as "tequila." Permission was granted. At the 1893 Chicago World's Fair, "mezcal de Tequila" won an award, and after that it was simply known as "tequila." The blue agave plant received a renaming as well when German naturalist Franz Weber came across the plant in his study of Mexican flora in 1896. The official name became *Agave tequilana Weber variedad azul*.

The 20th century was no less interesting in Mexico's booming tequila industry. It was now the national drink, a symbol of pride and prestige, and

A mechanized tahona wheel, an update on the traditional method of juicing agave

exports were increasing by the year. Distilleries continued to pop up throughout the countryside. The first distillery, El Centenario (home to today's Siete Leguas Tequila), in the highlands of Jalisco known as Los Altos, was established in 1910. Before the demise of President Porfirio Diaz's government, Jalisco would boast 87 distilleries, 32 of which lasted the government switch. Tequila was a prize for both sides during the revolution, part of the reward as the fight went back and forth with victories and defeats.

In the 1920s and '30s, more modern techniques like sanitary practices and cultivated yeasts were introduced to the tequila industry. During the 1930 outbreak of Spanish influenza, tequila with lime and salt was a common prescription given out by doctors and formed the foundation for the "lick-sip-suck" custom that remains in today's tequila shots.

When the United States' Prohibition of alcohol began in 1920, business was great for Mexicans in the tequila trade. Smuggling booze into the "dry" country was not limited to rum and whiskey, and a fair share of tequila made its way across the Rio Grande. Smugglers used any means available, and profits were high. Some of the accounts include airplanes that flew to the border states as well as individuals, horses, and burros packed with tequila crossing the river. One of those burros was rather smart. An article in *The New York Times* reports that in 1925, a donkey was led to Mexico by his owner, who left him at a house overnight to be packed with tequila. The donkey was led back to the river and returned, unattended, to his owner's home with the stash, avoiding human enemies (border authorities) along the way. Supposedly this burro made this journey quite often.

In Nogales, Arizona, a person seeking a drink need only walk across the street to Nogales, Sonora, to a saloon for a tipple of beer, wine, or tequila (no whiskey was allowed). However, the glory of the U.S. ban was short-lived for the tequila industry. In 1922, the *Bakersfield Californian* reported that the Mexican president was considering a prohibition in his own country to quell the tequila pipeline running to the north. This idea was thwarted by the promise of a farmers' rebellion. The boom really came to an end when the Great Depression hit both countries in 1929.

For as much as the tequila industry gained in the previous decades, it lost most of its good reputation in the years to follow. The 1930s saw a government land reform that split large estates, cutting cultivation by two-thirds. Between that and the economic crisis, just a handful of distilleries were left to struggle.

In the interest of business, and due to the agave shortage, a cheaper product was devised — the "mixto." Distillers began to add non-agave sugars, typically sugarcane, to the fermenting juices. This dilution was not too bad, and it was actually a better fit to the American palate, which preferred the less intense beverage. Exports grew once again and were fueled by World War II, when European liquors became unavailable. Postwar Mexico saw a decline in sales again as European markets improved. Sales within Mexico grew, however, due partly to an influx of Mexican films showing strong, macho heroes for whom tequila was the drink of choice.

In 1944, the labeling regulation was enacted that only tequila produced in Jalisco could be called "Tequila," and in 1949, the first official standard was placed on tequila, requiring it to be made entirely of agave. By 1964, however, the mixtos had their influence; up to 30% of non-agave sugars were permitted, and the first types were recognized, though this was limited to blanco and añejo (reposado was recognized in 1968). This eventually grew to the current 49% in 1970, but at that time the differentiation of 100% blue agave was also a standard. Through all of this, Tequila Herradura was the only distillery to retain 100% blue agave in its tequila.

The current Appellation of Origin and NOM regulations came into effect in 1974. These protected tequila's name as a product of Mexico and defined the current regions of the country where it is permitted to be produced. The 1960s and '70s were great for tequila. Sauza and Cuervo made up 60% of the market, the margarita was the top cocktail in the United States, and tourism and the 1968 Olympics in Mexico City gave the world a taste of tequila, which they took home. An article in a 1972 edition of the *Eugene Register-Guard* (Oregon) reported that in the "last 10 years production has soared from 300,000 liters annually to 4.2 million liters." There was a catch, though. Tequila producers knew that they could not keep up with this demand year after year.

Drinkers got a taste of premium tequilas, and they liked it. In 1983, Chinaco fueled this newfound taste for the good stuff by marketing its tequila as being as fine as Cognac. Tequila producers found themselves with a demand for quality, 100% blue agave tequila, which required more agave than the mixtos that had been so popular for decades, and what was to come in the '90s would not help the situation. Already short on stock of mature agave, farmers were waiting the 8–12 years needed to harvest some of their crops. Price wars ensued as agave prices grew, demand from drinkers was at an all-time high, and then the crops were hit by a deep freeze and relentless fungus. All of the elements of a crisis were in place.

In the few decades since, the tequila industry persevered and became better as a whole. Today's tequila industry is healthy and strong and seeing an unbelievable increase every year.

Harvested agave piñas

index